BAGGING
THE BUNNY

Published by Randall R. Bresee at CreateSpace

CreateSpace Edition: ISBN-978-0-9913047-2-1

Cover Design by http://www.ebooklaunch.com

BAGGING THE BUNNY

by

Randall R Bresee

Dedication

This book is dedicated to the person who brought me life and taught me to be free. My mother exposed me to the wonderful world that awaits people who don't take themselves too seriously. She also taught me that people can paint their lives brightly and boldly through wit, half-wit, adventure and lighthearted fun. I couldn't have asked for a better mom. Thank you, Jeb.

Contents

Introduction

A personal account of growing up during the idealistic 1950's and entering adulthood during the 1960's is provided through true stories about people who use wit, half-wit and a sense of adventure to tackle life's challenges. Hilarious failures and uplifting successes show that everyday activities provide people with opportunities to paint their lives brightly and boldly. This is the first book in a series that tells memorable stories of real people who deal with life in heartwarming and humorous ways as they approach life with unashamed zeal.

CHAPTER 1

A Friendly Canasta Game

My father was a handsome young man who served as the navigator and bombardier in a B-25 bomber during World War II. He was grateful to leave the air force while still in one piece and, like most young soldiers who survived the battles, set about trying to regain a normal life with his beautiful young wife when the war wound down. His first few years after the war were dedicated to finishing college and then moving to Bartlesville, Oklahoma to begin a new job. My mother was a glamorous, intelligent woman who was full of life and made their house in Bartlesville into a warm home filled with lighthearted fun and adventure.

The years after the war saw my parent's path frequently crossing those of people they had met during the war. Those encounters often occurred by chance and led to hearty social activities which seemed to have no goal other than to celebrate life itself. It was during one of those social activities in Bartlesville that I came into the world as a post-war baby boomer.

The "Labor" March

My mother thought it was uncanny how the war brought people together from all over the country and then sent them on their separate ways after the war only to bump into each other again and again in later years. During one evening in 1949, my parents were playing canasta in their Bartlesville living room with two other couples they had met during the war. Everyone was having a splendid time as evidenced by the laughter and kidding that joyfully filled the room.

Money was in short supply so small but nevertheless important bets were waged to make the card game more interesting. On this particular night, my parents enjoyed a prolonged winning streak and their financial gain was building impressively by the minute. The pile of coins and paper accumulating in front of them was welcome indeed, especially with their third child on the way. As the winnings grew my parents enjoyed teasing others about their losses. The banter from all sides of the table was spirited and warm.

My mother had been through child birth twice before so she knew the pains that she felt during the card game were serious. However, she kept them to herself since everyone was having such great fun. She remained quiet about her contractions and my parents impressive winning streak continued. After several more episodes of labor pain, however, she whispered to my father that the game might have to be cut short. He was excited by their winnings and was a little disappointed that my mother had begun labor. He delicately argued that she had previously been through two relatively uneventful births so they should keep playing canasta a while longer. The game continued and my parents winnings grew even more.

After a few more hands were played, my mother involuntarily informed everyone at the table that her contractions could not be ignored any longer. That occurred when a particularly sharp pain caused her to grip the table with her hands and pull herself to her feet. It was such a sudden and unexpected movement that others unconsciously gripped the table when she did. Everyone watched silently for a minute as they waited for my mother to provide information about her condition.

One woman finally asked, "Are you feeling a bad pain?" My mother calmly joked, "Yes, it's from you losing so much money!" Then she quipped, "It's so easy taking your cash that I'd rather be at a movie watching Orson Welles and Alida Valli in 'The Third Man' than playing cards here with all of you jokers." Everyone laughed and she sat back down. As was typical for those days, people acted as though nothing had happened and no one uttered a word about the incident.

The game resumed and plenty of lighthearted humor was exchanged among all of the players. My mother's contractions continued but she absorbed them without making a sound. Eventually a wave of quick pains flowed over her and she was fairly certain that she had to get to the hospital immediately or a child would be born in the living room. The desperate look on her face convinced everyone that it was time to run to the hospital.

"Run" was not literally correct because they walked. The hospital was located four blocks away and none of the players owned a car large enough to seat all six people so the group decided it would be simpler to make the trip on foot. No one perceived walking to be a problem since there was plenty of help for my mother during the journey. As they began their trek, one of the players turned to my mother and said, "I can't believe you're so calm. Why aren't you moaning and groaning?" My mother joked in reply, "It's because I'm one of those fantastic Texans you are always hearing about!"

The group slowly made their way toward the hospital while they continued to laugh and kid one another. My mother enthusiastically participated in the chatter and launched her share of witty barbs. Periodically during their walk, however, contractions caused her to stiffen and stop walking. The others held her up until the labor pains subsided. Then, laughter and kidding started again as if nothing had happened. At one point, one of the men sheepishly admitted that he was having trouble during the labor pains. My mother jested, "You're lucky it's not raining on us. Can you see me dodging raindrops on the way to the hospital?" Another man gulped and replied, "I hope this is the last baby we have." My mother later said she thought it was humorous that "we" six were having a baby.

Many years later, I stared at my mother with admiration as she told me that she delighted in the banter and jokes which were exchanged during their "hike" to the hospital. Imagine someone being witty and truly enjoying chatting with friends while enduring labor pains as she walked to the hospital only minutes before delivering a child. My mother also told me that she seriously worried they might not arrive at the hospital soon enough. Fortunately, they reached their destination in time but with only a few moments to spare.

Unforeseen encounters with wartime acquaintances years after the war ended sometimes delivered a surprise when it was least expected. When the group arrived at the hospital, my mother and father were shocked to see a familiar face in the maternity ward. They had met the man during a rest and relaxation period in California which was offered to airmen and their spouses when active duty ended as the war wound down. Numerous social activities were provided at that time to help people make the transition from soldier to civilian.

A dance had been scheduled as one of those social activities and my parents were seated at one end of a long table that was crowded with many others. As she frequently was known to do, my mother kicked off her shoes under the table. Unknown to her, other people collected her shoes and passed them to the far end of the table. Shortly after that happened, a doctor my parents had just met earlier in the evening walked to the back of my mother's chair and asked her to dance. She happily agreed and reached for her shoes but they were not located where she had put them. While she looked all around her chair, she explained the situation to the doctor. They both searched but the shoes simply weren't there. My mother could sense that mischief was in the air and informed the doctor that she suspected foul play had occurred. My mother and the man were determined to find her shoes.

They widened their search and eventually found themselves crawling under the table on their hands and knees. Of course, people were amused and numerous wisecracks erupted as the two wiggled and squirmed around the legs of others seated at the table. The fun lasted until my mother and the doctor crawled all the way to the other end of the long table where they located their bounty. The two finally danced and everyone at the table had good, lighthearted fun as the evening wore on. After the dance ended, my parents never saw the doctor again.

That is, until the night my mother and the canasta group walked into the maternity ward of the Bartlesville hospital. The doctor on duty was the man who had crawled under the table with my mother in California several years earlier.

Everyone immediately began catching-up on life since the war ended. The conversation included my parent's string of good luck during the canasta game that night as well as stories of other card games long ago. Talk was fast and cheerful and the doctor actually leaned on my mother's stomach at one point so he could hear a story better. My mother said she enjoyed listening to the laughter and lighthearted repartee as everyone had a great time reliving stories.

After several more minutes, my good-natured mother informed everyone that the baby was beginning its journey. In those days, it was common to administer anesthesia to women to render them unconscious during childbirth. The last thing my mother remembered while descending into unconsciousness was the doctor retelling the story about how he and she retrieved her lost shoes under the long table in California during the war. I entered the world a few minutes later.

I was lucky to have been born into an environment of warmth, friendship, laughter and lighthearted fun. I'd have to say that I am proud to have joined the world in the midst of hearty social activity that had no goal other than to celebrate life itself.

More Children Followed

As the years passed, more Bresee children were brought into the world until nine kids filled our house. My mother assumed the responsibility of naming children in our family. As was her usual approach to things, she enjoyed the task and did a good job choosing names.

Farrar Ann, the first child, was named after Farrar Storm, a young woman who attended high school with our mother in Houston, Texas. Our mother described Ms Storm as the "Queen of the High School" and said that she was talented, extremely beautiful and liked by all.

The second child, Kirk Palmer, was named after the handsome and rugged actor, Kirk Douglas. Palmer was our father's middle name.

I was the third child. Our mother has been an avid reader all of her life and named me Randall Richard to honor a protagonist in a novel by Ben Ames Williams, an American writer who published more than thirty books.

The fourth child, Keith Michael, was named after the principle character in a novel by Thomas Costain, a Canadian writer best known for historical novels. The character, Keith Alexander, was known as the "Black Knight of Vengeance." Our mother said the guy was kick-ass, liked his liquor and was a lady-killer.

The fifth child, Nicholas Kyle, was named after Kyle Rote, an All-American collegiate football star in Texas during the late 1940's and early 1950's. Our mother thought Mr. Rote was ruggedly handsome, intelligent and manly.

The sixth child was named Lucinda Lenore after another character in a Ben Ames Williams novel.

Alida Caroline was the seventh child. She was named after Alida Valli, a noted Italian film star from "The Third Man." Our mother noted that Alida Valli was beautiful, talented and a wonderful person.

Careen Christine, the eighth child, was named after a character in the popular novel, "Gone with the Wind."

Franklin Peter, the last child, was named to honor our father's father.

Our mother did a good job choosing names and most of them roll off the tongue quite nicely when vocalized. However, things never remained simple in our family, regardless of how good they were, so "nick names" evolved for many years.

Kirk renamed himself "Franklin Stringfellow" to respect a scout who served Robert E. Lee during the Civil War. Franklin's knowledge of terrain caused him to be designated the "most dangerous man in the Confederate army." Franklin fled to Canada immediately after the war and returned later to the U.S.A. to become an ordained minister.

When Keith was little, our mother called him "Monroe" because he sported platinum blond hair like Marilyn Monroe. A few years later, Keith adopted the name, "Drake Raines" which was a name he admired on a tombstone near Livingston, Texas. Just to confuse things a little more, my brother Kirk (i.e. Franklin Stringfellow) sometimes calls Keith, "Billy."

Lucinda added to the confusion by changing novels. As stated previously, our mother took Lucinda Lenore from a character in a Ben Ames Williams novel. Later, Lucinda adopted the name, "Suellen," after a character in the novel, "Gone with the Wind."

Alida has become known as "Owl." No one seems to remember the reason for that other than laziness by shortening a three syllable name to a single syllable. Alida also goes by the name "Hoot" for obvious reasons.

Franklin has become "Jedediah Hotchkiss" to honor the most famous mapmaker of the Civil War era. To make matters more interesting, Franklin discovered that our family is actually related to Jedediah Hotchkiss.

I renamed myself "Black Jack Logan" to honor a southern sympathizer who joined the Union army when the Civil War began. The turncoat distinguished himself repeatedly during the war and rose to the rank of Major General.

One of the odd things about our family is the amusement derived by the purposeful introduction of confusion to things that are simple. Imagine how much confusion occurs when someone in our family refers to "Franklin" during a conversation. This name could refer to my brother Kirk (Franklin Stringfellow) or my brother Franklin Peter. On numerous occasions confusion during conversations has caused such hardy laughter that tears were shed as family members struggled to identify who was who so they could understand a person's comments.

The Stage Was Set For 1950's Idealism

For many years after World War II ended, people were reminded frequently of the awful losses the war had inflicted. These reminders sometimes arose unexpectedly as was the case in 1948, a year before I was born. My parents drove past an airfield near Bartlesville with my older sister and brother when they saw several WW II planes parked on the tarmac. Since our father had served in the Air

Force, they decided to stop and admire the airplanes. Once they were close, they saw that the planes had received little attention since being parked when the war ended. That was easy to understand since the entire country was busy trying to get life back to normal.

Airport security was practically nonexistent back then so my father asked my mother to sit in the cockpit of a plane while he took a photograph. My mother cheerfully climbed onto the wing and made her way toward the fuselage. As she eased into the pilot's seat, she saw that dried blood coated much of the plane's interior. The ghastly condition of the plane sent shivers up her spine and revived terrible visions of war and the many friends who had died in awful ways far from home. As she told me this story many years later, her lips curled downward like she might get sick and she remarked, "The cockpit smelled like death." After the photo was taken, she was anxious to exit and lost no time climbing out of the airplane.

Hearing that story helped me understand the 1950's and early 1960's better. With the horrors of WW II fresh in the mind of nearly every adult, it was reasonable that people tried to get as far from those experiences as they could. It is easy to see how people's tastes and behavior tended toward idealism such as that displayed by the Cleaver family in the "Leave It to Beaver" television series.

In other words, the extremes of WW II led to a rebound which evolved into the extraordinary idealism of the 1950's and early 1960's. This made me feel a little odd when I recognized that I grew up in an era that was full of hope, optimism and renewal but which resulted from a great and horrible war.

CHAPTER 2

Our House Had Magic

If there is one place where Santa Claus, the Easter Bunny and other miraculous events should be celebrated, it is a family with numerous young children. Luckily for the Bresee kids, our parents went to great lengths to create a magical atmosphere at times that are important to young children. Read the following stories and decide if you would have believed in miracles if you had been a young child in our family.

Right On, Virginia

Holiday excitement started building a month before Christmas at our house when our mother began amassing an enormous inventory of Christmas cookies. She baked every conceivable kind of cookie – white, brown, green, beige, powdery, sticky, chocolate, ginger, rum, round and flat. Most family members had a favorite cookie and our mother managed to bake everyone's favorite plus many others. She literally baked thousands of cookies and recorded the cookie count on a list. The smallest batch I recall her baking at one time was four dozen. When yet another batch was finished, the type and number of cookies were added to her list. Teachers at school learned about our mother's cookie-baking feat and periodically asked us kids for updated cookie counts beginning at Thanksgiving. We reported cookie counts of, say, 1,360 one day and 2,188 two weeks later. Teachers couldn't believe it.

Cookies were reserved for Christmas Eve and they needed to be hidden from hungry hands for a month. Of course, the hands of little children were a concern but they only needed to be reminded that Santa would not visit children who misbehaved. The real threat to amassing a suitable cookie count by Christmas Eve was our father. He could devour fifty delicious cookies in one sitting without blinking an eye. Our mother needed to hide her treasures cleverly to prevent him from eating them faster than she could bake them.

As usual, she was up to the task. Her strategy was based on the different roles of men and women during the 1950's. Women usually cooked and cleaned the house whereas men performed other chores so our mother's cookie-hiding strategy was based on this division of labor.

The only cookies she stored in the freezer were ones she knew our father disliked. All other cookies were hidden in "women" places that he was unlikely to search. Our clever mother hid cookies in the kitchen oven, the washing machine, the dishwasher, and behind the floor length curtains of our parent's bedroom. Years later, my mother chuckled as she recalled her cookie-hiding campaign, "Dick was literally surrounded by thousands of cookies and he didn't know it." Watching my mother devise simple and effective solutions to problems taught me a lot.

Another key ingredient of the holidays was the arrival of the Christmas tree. We always had a freshly cut tree that was tall enough to nearly touch the living room ceiling.

After the tree was set in place, more than a dozen strings of blinking or bubbling colored lights were woven through its branches. Next, several dozen strings of colored antique glass beads were carefully draped over limbs. Hundreds of delicate antique glass ornaments along with all types, colors and sizes of new ornaments were hung on nearly every available part of the tree. Ornaments made by small children in previous years found their special places on the tree. Finally, glittering tinsel was draped over limbs like dangling icicles after a blizzard. The tree always looked sensational. That was somewhat astonishing to me considering that nine little pairs of hands did most of the decorating.

Another important ingredient of holiday spirit was music. Our parents enjoyed music and owned lots of records along with a good stereo system to play them. We had many of the classic Christmas albums including Bing Crosby, Frank Sinatra, Perry Como, Nat Cole, the Ray Conniff Singers, the Billy Vaughn Orchestra and the Bert Kaempfert Orchestra. After the tree was decorated, most evenings found family members sitting in the living room with all lights turned off except for the tree lights. We listened to Christmas albums for the zillionth time while smelling the freshly cut tree and admiring the dazzling decorations for hours. It was spectacular.

When Christmas Eve day finally arrived, we children recognized it as the most special day of the year and began preparing for Santa's arrival as soon as we crawled out of bed that morning. The fighting and raucous play that is typical of children miraculously ceased that day. Without prompting by our parents, essentially all normal kids' activities stopped at noon and children disappeared to their bedrooms. We knew this was a really important day in terms of our behavior and we could not afford to give Santa a reason to skip our house. If our bid to please Santa was successful, we could look forward to staying awake all night playing with marvelous toys that he left us. We rested through the day as much as we could. Children hardly made a sound as they remained in their beds and napped in anticipation of a long night of play.

The electricity of quiet anticipation wafted through the air of our home all day long. Our mother said many years later that Christmas Eve day was her favorite day of the year because the atmosphere was completely different from all other days. While we children remained quietly in our rooms to avoid conflicts and rest for a long night of play, our mother was free to work with almost no interruptions. She said the environment reminded her of stories she read about Christmas during Victorian times. It was magical.

Santa visited our home on Christmas Eve and our parents devised an enchanting way to marshal him in. Beginning early in the evening, the radio was tuned to a station that periodically reported Santa's location. After speculating about his route for several hours, our father declared that Santa seemed to be traveling in our direction and it was time to search for him in the neighborhood.

Our mother always claimed that she needed to care for an ill neighbor or didn't feel well herself and needed to remain home. Even though she said this every year, we children did not find it to be suspicious. We repeatedly warned our mother that she must stay out of sight and remain very quiet. We reminded her that it was especially important not to walk around the house because she might startle

Santa before he finished leaving presents. Of course, we possessed short memories and were so excited that our minds were devoid of anything but thoughts of Santa and the presents he might soon leave.

When we children felt that we had our mother under control, we piled into the car with our father. He drove through the neighborhood slowly while numerous pairs of little eyes scanned rooftops and lawns for sleigh tracks and reindeer hoof prints. We listened to the car radio at a barely audible sound to hear more reports of Santa's location being announced. The low radio sound was used to avoid disturbing Santa if he was in the neighborhood nearby.

The cold air was still and quiet as children opened car windows to listen for the sound of sleigh bells in the night. After driving for half an hour or so, we drove to the highest hill in the area to get a better view of the night sky. Our father shut off the car engine as we sat quietly to listen carefully for sleigh bells while we scanned the sky for Rudolph's bright red nose. After about twenty minutes, our father declared that he thought he heard bells and saw a blinking red light in the sky. Children began to get extremely excited at that point.

With fresh evidence that Santa might be close, we started the car and searched the neighborhood again. We drove near our house but were careful to remain a block away to avoid startling Santa in case he was there. Children did not know that the purpose of this maneuver was to allow our father to determine if our mother had finished placing gifts under the tree. When her work was completed, our mother raised a particular window shade that could be seen from a block away. When our father saw the shade raised, he would drive around the neighborhood once more. During this last trip, he declared that he definitely heard sleigh bells or definitely got a glimpse of reindeer on a rooftop.

By this time, children were getting hysterical and it wouldn't take long for a child to cry out that he saw Santa Claus. When I was a first grader, I clearly saw Santa on the roof of a house as it somehow opened up to drop him inside. At least one child saw Santa every year. After he was spotted, our father proclaimed that he saw Santa, too. That was enough encouragement to cause all of the children to shout that they heard reindeer snorting or saw them stomping their hooves in the snow. Our father stepped on the gas and we raced home as fast as we could. When we arrived, our father cautioned that Santa might not have finished leaving presents under the tree and we should guard against startling him before his work was completed.

We agreed that the best strategy for dealing with this situation was to send the smallest child who could walk to evaluate the situation. The lucky child carefully made his way to the front porch to peer through a low living room window while the rest of us waited anxiously in the car. In my mind, I can still see a little child taking this task very seriously while working his way up the sidewalk before raising up on tiptoes to look through the window. Upon seeing the delightful sight under the tree, the child invariably yelled, "He's been here! Santa's been here!"

The remaining children screamed while exploding from the car like bullets discharged from a high powered rifle. We sped up the sidewalk as fast as our little legs would churn and burst into the house. Children were initially mesmerized as their eyes feasted on the sensational scene that awaited them. What a sight to behold!

Imagine the number of presents that nine children received at Christmas. Beneath beautiful lights and ornaments of a dazzling tree, the floor was literally filled with presents wrapped in colorful paper and bright ribbon. Presents included bicycles, school clothes, cap guns, Lincoln Logs, Erector Sets, Tinker Toys, dolls, tennis rackets, baseball gloves, train sets and just about everything a child can imagine. With so many children in our family, someone received a bicycle or train set every year.

Nine excited children engaged in a frenzied battle for floor space as they located and opened their gifts from Santa. Paper and ribbons were ripped off packages in seconds and screams of joy filled the room.

When the initial surge of opening presents slowed, children migrated to the kitchen to begin the feast that had awaited them for more than a month. Christmas cookies were special and we were allowed to eat as many as we wanted on Christmas Eve. Children remained awake most of the night enjoying their presents, admiring the colorful tree and listening to classic Christmas music while devouring delicious cookies until nearly getting sick and then eating more after a brief rest. It was enchanting.

To this day, I can clearly remember the sights, smells and sounds of Christmas Eve in our home. Ah, what a magical scene. I certainly believe that the New York Sun was correct in 1897 when it reported, "Yes, Virginia, there is a Santa Claus."

Ammo Fell Through The Ceiling

With five boys and several tomboys in the family, Santa nearly always left us toy weapons. They included Winchester rifles, numerous types of cowboy pistols and holsters, a World War II era Browning automatic rifle, a derringer mounted in a belt buckle that fired when a person pushed out his stomach and many other toy guns. Our weapons cache allowed us to perfect trick shooting, quick drawing, surprise attacks and raw intimidation. We were formidable cowboys, Indians, civil war soldiers or World War II infantrymen.

Nearly all of our guns required ammunition and caps were the preferred ammo in the 1950's and 1960's. Each child who received a new gun also received a box of caps. As you might expect, the gun battles fought on Christmas Eve were fast and furious and ammunition was quickly spent.

Fortunately, our father had a mystical source that resupplied our ammunition caches. After a suitable amount of cajoling, he would begin searching for "vibrations" in the air. While reaching toward the ceiling and waving both hands, our father searched for air pockets that revealed the presence of the magical vibrations. When he located vibrations that were strong enough, he began chanting, "Abra-Cadabra-Do" over and over again as he waved his hands more vigorously with each chant.

Small children with eyes opened wide stared at the ceiling for signs of vibrations and became increasingly excited as our father's chanting was repeated louder and louder. We didn't know how, but we knew that the ceiling would open and boxes of caps would drop through the air. As our father chanted louder and louder, he suddenly lurched forward and seemed to push the air apart as boxes of caps flew directly into his hands.

How mystical that event was! I distinctly remember seeing the ceiling open on several occasions as our father retrieved box after box of ammunition for our toy guns. Although he nearly always wore short sleeved shirts at home, we children never noticed that he changed into a long sleeved shirt immediately before conducting this magical feat. Unknown to us, the real flight path of caps into his hands was from a location between his shirt cuff and wrist.

Seeing caps drop from the ceiling added to the miraculous wonder of Christmas Eve. We children were lucky to experience such wondrous times. I believe that the active imaginations which many of us Bresees' retain to this day began when our childhood eyes were opened wide and magic filled the air.

Bagging The Bunny

Easter was another marvelous time at our house. Like many other families, our mother dressed her children in elegant clothes for Sunday School on Easter. The girls wore dresses with white gloves and carried handbags. Boys wore white shirts, coats and ties. Our parents took photographs of children in their Easter outfits to acquire a good record of each child's growth. I often wondered how our mother managed to dress so many children and get them to Sunday school on time.

Each child in our family had his own Easter basket. I still have my old basket with my name written across its top. We also constructed Easter "nests" in the yard outside using wild onion stems which emerged in early spring. Our mother hardboiled many dozens of eggs and we decorated them with food dye, wax, colored foil, crayons or any other material we could lay our hands on.

Baskets were placed along a wall of the dining room before going to bed and the first child who awakened on Easter morning rushed to the baskets to see if the Easter Bunny had arrived. A loud scream informed everyone in the house that chocolates, candy, colored eggs and other indulgences filled our baskets. Onion stem nests in the yard also were filled with delicious delicacies. Children feasted until they could eat no more. It was great.

I was one of the "Bigs" since I was the third of nine children. As the Bigs grew older, they helped our mother by dispensing delights into the "Middles" and "Littles" baskets after they fell asleep. I had been enchanted by the Easter Bunny's visit for many years and was happy to help pass this pleasure to my younger brothers and sisters. One spring, it was more challenging than usual.

My brother Nick was four years younger than me. He was old enough to hear some classmates at school remark that the Easter Bunny didn't really exist and claim that Easter treats were simply supplied by parents. At home, we told Nick that the kids at school were wrong. Nick thought about it for a long time and decided to resolve this dilemma with a test to determine once and for all if the Easter Bunny was real or merely a contrivance of well-meaning but deceptive parents.

Nick devised a test which consisted of two parts. First, he told us that he would construct his wild onion nest outside as usual but would place it in a secret location far from the house without disclosing its location to anyone. He reasoned that, if the Easter Bunny was real, it could locate the nest and leave treats. If his classmates claims were correct that parent chicanery was the real source of Easter treats, Nick's outdoor nest would remain empty on Easter morning since its location was known only to himself. Nick secretly constructed his nest without being seen and announced that it was finished three days before Easter.

Our mother asked me to search the neighborhood to locate Nick's nest. Since our wild onion nests typically were about one foot in diameter and only two inches high, finding it was a real challenge. I mapped out the neighborhood on a grid and began searching areas closest to the house first and then methodically expanded my search gridline-by-gridline to include areas farther away. On my second full day of arduous searching, I located Nick's nest more than an eighth of a mile from the house on the side of a large gully. The nest was cleverly concealed between a log and stump and was shrouded with brush. All we needed to do was fill it with treats at the appropriate time and we had an answer for the first part of Nick's test. Whew, my mother and I felt relief.

The second part of Nick's test was a bit trickier. Nick reasoned that the only sure way to prove to his classmates that the Easter Bunny actually existed was to take the bunny to school to show the non-believers. Nick's plan was to shoot the bunny with his BB gun and carry its carcass to school as unequivocal proof that the Easter Bunny actually existed.

As usual, Easter baskets were placed along the wall of the dining room early during the evening before Easter. A small room used as a library was located off the opposite side of the dining room. After all of the other children went to bed and the house became quiet, Nick set up his post in the library. He turned out the lights, partially closed the door between the library and dining room and began watching. Only the barrel of his BB gun stuck through the small opening of the doorway.

My mother and I were certain that Nick could not remain awake for very long. However, we didn't know that he prepared for his nighttime mission by taking a long nap earlier in the day. We waited and waited and waited. Many hours passed and we feared Nick would never fall asleep. We were ready to admit defeat and we quietly discussed how we would explain that the Easter Bunny was nothing more than a ruse.

Luckily, Nick fell asleep an hour and a half before sunrise. My mother quickly placed treats in the baskets along the dining room wall while I grabbed a flashlight and carried treats outside to fill the onion nests in the yard. I sprinted through light rain to the gully and filled Nick's hidden nest with a particularly large number of colorful eggs and chocolates.

The indoor baskets were filled by the time I returned from the gully so my mother and I quietly reveled in our success. We noticed that I had tracked mud onto the linoleum floor and then we suddenly realized that we had an opportunity to decisively boost Nick's conviction that the Easter Bunny was real.

Nick enjoyed wildlife and the outdoors and had begun learning to identify animal sounds and animal tracks. Of course, he never actually saw photographs of Easter Bunny tracks in his reference books but he knew what normal rabbit tracks looked like. So did I.

My mother quickly wiped up my muddy footprints while I dashed outside to fill a small bowl with mud. When back inside, I dipped three fingers into the mud, held them close together to form a triangle and pressed my fingers against the linoleum to make a footprint that looked similar to a rabbit footprint. The print looked good so I began making tracks as fast as I could. When we were finished, muddy tracks on the floor seemed to show that the Easter Bunny entered the house through the back door near the dining room, hopped to each basket and then exited out the dining room window. We smiled at each other while admiring our work for a few minutes and then slipped off to bed.

Nick woke shortly after the sun rose and immediately peered through the library door to see Easter baskets overflowing with treats. He raced to get a close look at the baskets and quickly detected fresh tracks on the floor. He studied them carefully and concluded that whatever made the tracks had entered through the back door and exited out the window. His eyes were open wide as he explained that he didn't know for sure, but the tracks looked like they were Easter Bunny tracks. Then, Nick remembered his onion nest hidden in the gully and raced to check it. He found his nest overflowing with colored eggs and chocolates.

There was no question about it - Nick was a believer. Although he did not have a bunny carcass to show his classmates at school as he hoped, Nick went to school the next day confident that the Easter Bunny indeed was real. I think Nick believed in the Easter Bunny almost to adulthood. Children can be such great fun.

CHAPTER 3

Life During The 1950's and 1960's

When I turned one year old in 1950, my father's employer transferred him from Bartlesville, Oklahoma to Saint Louis, Missouri. Like many other cities, new neighborhoods were developed in Saint Louis to provide housing for the America's booming postwar population. Our family filled an 1,100 square foot house in a new neighborhood that had lots and lots of children. The house was small by today's standards but our parents were simply grateful to live in a solid, new house.

This chapter provides a few stories that will help many readers better understand life in the 1950's. Naturally, our family had its own way of dealing with life's basic challenges.

A Fine House

Imagine cooking and serving meals for eleven people in a tiny kitchen that measured only 10 feet by 12 feet. In spite of space limitations, our mother didn't think it was a problem and her children's bodies were fortified with freshly prepared meals that were healthy and included lots of vegetables. I think the nine Bresee children were fortunate compared to many of today's "fast food" children.

Having enough bedroom space for eleven people in an 1,100 square foot house was more challenging. Our father worked in the unfinished attic to provide two bedrooms and a bathroom for the older children. My older sister slept in one bedroom and four boys slept in a larger bedroom. The attic wasn't constructed tightly and outside light streamed through cracks around windows. Attic space was unheated and heat was supplied by opening the door at the bottom of the stairs to allow warm air to flow upward. It was cold during winters and we slept under a pile of wool "army" blankets to keep warm. I remember my toes being squashed by the weight of heavy wool blankets. The blankets felt good, however.

The bare wood floor of the attic tormented us with splinters when we played. Our father eventually placed pieces of used carpet on the main floor areas when it became evident that getting carpet would be less trouble than pulling splinters out of children's feet and elbows. Overall, there were few complaints and the attic seemed to be comfortable.

The clothes washer and dryer were located in the basement. Disposable diapers did not exist in the 1950's and nine children dirtied plenty of fabrics so our mother washed about nine loads of laundry each day. That adds up to a lot of trips carrying laundry up and down the basement stairs. Permanent press fabrics were not invented yet and our mother set up her ironing board in the living room each Monday to iron for about eight hours. People worked

hard in the 1950's and my mother worked harder than anyone I knew.

Trips To The Grocery Store

Our family made one grand trip to the grocery store
each week. It was exciting as children piled into the car
and we drove to Kroger on Saturday night. One grocery basket was filled with bread and milk while everything else
was put into three other baskets. Most kids wanted to help
push a grocery basket and each child got a turn. Of course,
the "littles" couldn't push a heavy basket very well so our
movement down the aisles could be quite slow. The spectacle of our large family inching through the store must have
looked like a four-car convoy winding down a narrow road
overrun by a herd of small two-legged critters. Although
we were well-behaved, strangers must have thought that it
was impossible for our parents to watch all of us kids well
enough. Actually, that was correct.

Check-out at grocery stores in the 1950's took a long
time since there were no bar code scanners, self check-
out stations and devices to swipe credit cards. As items
were unloaded from baskets, the cashier read each price
tag before manually punching its cost into a cash regis-
ter. Checking-out our mother's four baskets of groceries
typically required about thirty minutes so I often walked
around the store to look at things while she checked-out.
As has often been the case during my life, I lost track of
time. And our parents lost track of me. When check-out was
completed, the family loaded grocery bags into the station
wagon and drove home.

Meanwhile, I continued to wander until I reasoned

that it was time to return to the check-out area. I discovered that no family members were in sight. I sprinted to the parking lot and saw that the family car was absent from its parking space.

I observed a bench outside the grocery store and calmly took a seat to wait, knowing that my absence would be discovered eventually. I simply watched people and waited while more than an hour passed before my absence at home was noticed. My parents deduced that I had not been in the car during the trip home so they drove back to the grocery store. When I saw them drive into the parking lot, I calmly walked to the curb and waited. My parents also were calm and the incident was not a big deal for any of us. Growing up in a large family tends to help parents and children gain a perspective which alleviates panic at times that upset many other people. There indeed are benefits to being part of a big family.

People in large families tend to be more resourceful than others, largely out of necessity. Occasionally, our father drove our mother and children to the grocery store and then returned home to work. When our mother was nearly finished checking out, she used the pay telephone to call our father at home. Our family developed a signal to eliminate the "expensive" cost of using the pay telephone since saving a nickel was worth a little effort in those days.

Pay telephones returned a caller's money if the call was not answered so our parents took advantage of that feature by communicating without actually answering the telephone. Our mother inserted a nickel into the grocery store telephone, dialed home, let the phone ring twice and then hung up. Her nickel was returned. She reinserted the nickel, dialed again, let the phone ring twice and hung up again. Two rings followed by two more rings was our father's signal to pick up our mother at the grocery store. No one at home answered the telephone unless it rang more than twice so the signal was communicated without cost.

Another fun part of Saturday night grocery jaunts occurred when we returned home. We seldom ate cookies or watched television in our house but we did both after returning from the grocery store. We children opened a package of cookies and sat in front of a snowy black and white television so our mother could put away groceries with few interruptions. Most of our favorite programs were westerns and the highlight of Saturday night was "Gunsmoke," a western set in 1880's Dodge City, Kansas. We admired the brave and unflinching U.S. Marshall, Matt Dillon, and dreamed of riding his fine horse, Marshall.

During the introduction of Gunsmoke episodes, Marshall Dillon stood tall in the street and drew his six-gun against a bad guy. We eagerly anticipated this event by strapping on our six-shooters and waiting anxiously for the draw scene while bravely standing our ground in front of the television. We stared at the picture tube nervously as our fingers twitched while waiting for the moment Marshall Dillon went for his gun. At that instant, we attempted to out-draw Matt. Our manhood was measured by how close we came to beating him. Oh, the 1950's were exciting times!

Another Saturday night television hero we admired was the star of a program set in 1870's San Francisco. The hero of "Have Gun Will Travel" was a highly educated former army officer named Paladin who helped people who were unable to protect themselves. We were quite familiar with

Paladin's preferred firearm, a Colt 45 single action revolver with a 7.5 inch barrel and a one-ounce trigger pull. We respected his integrity and admired his proficiency with a six-gun. We all wanted a six-shooter like Paladin.

Saturday night television during the 1950's fed the dreams of innumerable young kids and helped develop their values. I suspect that many young children today dream of things that are far less healthy than protecting the people of Dodge City or helping distraught citizens of San Francisco who can't protect themselves.

Mohawks

As our mother put away groceries one Saturday night, we children watched a television program about Mohawk Indians. I always admired Indians and secretly wanted to be one. I was fascinated by how they lived close to nature and believed the Mohawk haircut was the neatest thing I ever saw. After watching this program, I would have given my right arm to have a haircut like them.

Our parents saved money by owning hair clippers that allowed our father to cut the kid's hair on weekends. Since the crew cut style was the only hair style that matched our father's expertise level, all five boys sported crew cuts. Our father frequently reminded us that "poor people have poor ways" and giving the boys a quick crew cut was a poor man's solution to five haircut problems.

After watching the television program about Mohawk Indians, my brothers and I begged our father to give us a Mohawk-style haircut instead of a crew cut. Our main argument was that playing cowboys and Indians would be easier if we sported Mohawk haircuts since we could be recognized as Indians more readily. He relented a few weekends later after realizing that Mohawk cuts were nearly as simple as crew cuts. A friend named Billy happened to be spending the weekend at our house and Billy asked if he could receive a Mohawk haircut, too. Our father had a twinkle in his eye as he informed Billy that we needed to get permission from his mother.

Our father telephoned Billy's mother. He said that he was giving the Bresee boys a haircut and he offered to cut Billy's hair, too. Billy's mother replied that our father's offer was very generous and she would be pleased if Billy received a haircut. Our father delicately asked if she had any special hair cutting instructions and Billy's mom replied, "No." Our father said okay and chuckled as he hung up the telephone.

Like the rest of us, Billy was delighted to receive a Mohawk haircut. I was particularly proud of my new hair style and thought it stirred the feeling that I actually had Native American blood flowing through my veins. It was truly exciting. We figured that we were the neatest boys in the world and we roamed the neighborhood all day playing cowboys and Indians.

We drove Billy home that night and our father departed quickly when Billy jumped out of the car rather than waiting until Billy got inside the house. By the time we arrived home, Billy's mother had telephoned our house in a furious rage. Our father calmly reminded her that she provided no special hair cutting instructions and added that Billy simply got the haircut that he wanted. In school on Monday, Billy told me about a substance I had never heard about - hair growth tonic. I also learned that Billy was never allowed to visit our home again. Both of our parents thought that the haircut incident was quite funny.

Punishment

In a small house occupied by many people, it was necessary to maintain order to keep things from getting out-of-hand. Our parents usually didn't hesitate to dole out punishment when needed and an example of that occurred one evening while eating dinner. After most people finished eating, my oldest sister, Farrar, and I began throwing food at each other. Our actions were seen and we were sent to the unfinished basement for punishment. The cats slept in the basement and we were told, "If you are going to act like animals, go down into the basement with the animals."

My sister and I sat on the bottom step of the stairs and discussed our situation. It didn't take long for us to become indignant about how poorly we had been treated so we decided to show our parents a thing or two by running away from home. We considered several possible destinations and decided that China was a good place to go.

Farrar assured me that she knew how to get to China. We felt confident about our plan and walked to the basement door. We excitedly opened the door to begin our journey but froze motionless while we stared at the darkness outside. We hadn't considered what to do when it got dark. We both mumbled a few words and quickly decided that we should leave for China the next morning after the sun came up. We returned to our seats on the bottom step and were sent to bed a short time later. Of course, the next morning everything was rosy again and we forgot about our China travel plan. It's funny how things can appear to be awfully bad at times but then change quickly.

Our parents made sure that we knew how vulgar life could become if we misbehaved badly enough to require punishment by the public legal system. A classmate's father was a fireman at a firehouse located across the street from our grade school and the firehouse contained a jail cell in its basement. The cell was dark, smelly, dank and absolutely filthy.

Our father took the older children to the firehouse one afternoon. The firemen were very nice to us and gave us a tour of the building. We eventually descended into the basement and looked through the bars of the jail cell. Our father asked if we wanted to see the inside of the cell and, with a mixture of reluctance and curiosity, we agreed to take a closer look at the cell. Once inside, a fireman slammed the door shut and we children were locked inside.

We knew instinctively that we were trapped in a terrible place. We panicked and began to scream and cry uncontrollably. The firemen quickly opened the jail door to release us and we ran out of the cell. I was really scared and remained that way for a long time. Our father explained that it was good that we knew jail was a bad place. He added that we needed to be accountable for our actions and bad behavior could put us in jail for a long time. It was a good lesson to learn.

Our parents had an effective strategy to deal with misbehavior at school. They simply had faith in the school system and adopted the view that children were guilty until proven innocent. The only time I can recall my father visiting grade school was on the first day of school. He took me to the principal's office, introduced himself and introduced me as a new pupil in the school. With me standing by his side, my father told the principal that he had permission to punish me whenever I did anything wrong. My father's message was communicated very clearly to me because I knew that he meant it.

I was never punished by the principal and believe that my parent's strategy was a big reason for that. It is sad that many parents today assume that the school must have done something wrong when their child gets in trouble.

Things Aren't So Serious

Our family moved to the small town of Vandalia, Illinois in 1961. Our house was located within the city limits and we also owned a 186 acre farm seven miles from town. We grew wheat, raised sheep and did many fun and foolish things at the farm. One morning, our father brought home a newborn lamb whose mother died during birth. He instructed us children to care for the newborn until it was big enough to return to the flock at the farm. A picket fence surrounded our yard which provided safe quarters for the lamb. At this time, our house accommodated nine children, two cats, a dog and, now, a lamb. Children, cats and the dog ran through the yard having great fun and, now, the lamb ran with them.

One summer afternoon, our father brought home a salesman from St. Louis for a barbecue meal. While the meat cooked on the grill outside, our father and the salesman sat in the kitchen discussing business as my mother prepared other dishes. Just when the big-city salesman tried to make a serious point for my father, a cat dashed through the kitchen with four squealing children and a barking dog in hot pursuit.

The salesman quit speaking as he turned his head

to watch the runners pass. The expression on his face changed to amazement when he saw a lamb running to bring up the rear in hurried chase. He regained his composure and returned to his important point when the group ran through the kitchen in the opposite direction. Our father yelled at them to quiet down and quit running in the house. Our mother suggested that everyone have a little something to eat to hold down their appetites until the barbecue was ready. Each child retrieved something off of the table and began enjoying their morsel. Since the room had finally gotten quiet again, the big-city man resumed his sales pitch.

The cat, dog and lamb were standing in the kitchen and their hunger must have been triggered by watching the children eat. Our animals were fed on a side porch just off of the kitchen so the three walked a few steps onto the porch to eat. As was typical at our house, the dog munched cat food, the cat headed straight for the lamb's sweet oats and the lamb chewed dry dog food.

The salesman was seated at the end of the kitchen table where he could see directly into the side porch about six feet away. He stopped making his sales pitch mid-sentence and focused on the feeding animals. He watched the spectacle in silence for a minute or two and finally remarked, "A lamb eats dog food, a cat eats lamb food and a dog eats cat food, all IN THE HOUSE."

The salesman sat up in his chair and looked dumbfounded as he declared that he wouldn't have believed it if he hadn't seen it with his own eyes. Ah, city people. They take most things way too seriously.

Times Have Changed

In the years following the war, couples were having lots of children and the size of the baby boom generation quickly grew. With few television programs and no computers or video games, most children spent their playtime outdoors. We walked to school like nearly all children and we rode our bicycles many miles after school. I remember running home from school as fast as possible so I could bicycle to some unknown street or play a game outside with other children. It was easy to start a game of kick ball or whiffle ball since children were everywhere.

An abundance of children distilled life into simple and sensible patterns. For example, most automobile drivers reduced their speed when entering residential neighborhoods because they expected children to be playing in the streets. People today are in such a hurry to get somewhere else that many drivers don't even slow down in school zones unless they fear a policeman is present. That is really unfortunate.

When our family moved to Vandalia, Illinois in 1961, telephone numbers were only three digits and it was necessary for callers to go through a telephone operator. Party lines were common and they provided nosy neighbors with plenty of opportunities to learn about other people's activities. Occasionally several busybodies listened simultaneously to a person's conversation.

I was discussing the old party telephone system many years later with a former high school classmate whose family had a party line with several other families. If any family on the party line received a telephone call, the phones in the other homes also rang. Each family was assigned a certain ring count to help identify the recipient of the call. Don recounted how the telephone rang with the number of rings for his family's line and, when he picked up the phone, he often heard several clicks as neighbors on the party line picked up to eavesdrop. During one call, Don's mother told his grandmother that she had plenty of tomatoes in her garden and a neighbor busybody just happened to call Don's mother the next morning to ask if she could spare any extra tomatoes.

Think how telephone communication has changed since that time. Imagine having to listen to other people's telephones ringing every time they received a call. Well, maybe things have not changed that much after all. Today we have to listen to an awful lot of other people's cell phones ringing and then we are forced to listen to their conversations.

Some towns were so small that they lack public places for people to interact socially. In those cases, post offices often served as an important gathering place for local residents. People often retrieved their mail from the post office at about the same time every day in order to catch up on gossip with people who did likewise.

The way things sometimes got done in these small post offices would surprise many people living in large metropolitan areas. I remember a post office in a tiny Illinois town about four miles from Vandalia. The Hagarstown post office was located in a corner of a one-room store named, "Wrights General Store." The man who was the store owner, manager, cashier, bookkeeper, stock boy, custodian and anything else the store needed also was the postal service employee.

When you walked into Wrights Store, you usually saw the store owner performing different tasks throughout the store while wearing a baseball-style cap on his head. If you told him that you needed to purchase a postage stamp, he walked to the corner where a small number of postal boxes and other postal items were located. As he stepped behind the counter of the postal area, he removed his baseball cap and placed an official U.S. Postal Service cap on his head. He conducted the postal business and, when finished, changed hats again as he stepped back into the counter.

Another little town contained a tiny but interesting post office. The first thing that caught my attention was the diminutive size of the building. The whole post office building looked like it wasn't a bit larger than 450 square feet. The other interesting thing about it was a clothes line strung behind the building which frequently held freshly washed clothes.

Multitasking while conducting government business was more common in those days than it is now. Combining tasks provided tiny towns with a way to acquire important assets like a post office. In turn, the post office served as a gathering place to socialize and conduct business. It is a shame that official business has to be done so officially now.

It also is a shame that child play has changed so much since then. During the 1950's and early 1960's, most children in our neighborhood played in the streets, rode bicycles miles from home and generally were free to explore unknown places. When I was only 12 years old, I frequently hiked several miles to the river bottom to camp alone for the weekend and nobody thought much of it.

One Saturday evening, my father looked around the

dinner table and noticed that I was absent. He asked if any-one knew where I was. My brother Kirk said that he saw me leave on Friday after school for a camping trip to the river bottom. My father said okay and the conversation ended.

When I returned from camping on Sunday at dark, my father calmly asked what I had been doing all weekend. I told him that I hiked to the river bottom, set up camp and watched wildlife as I had done on other occasions. He asked for more details so I explained that I left my camp-site at daybreak and crawled into a dense thicket at the edge of a lake where I sat without moving a muscle for many hours. Few animals were aware of my presence so I could observe birds, turtles, snakes, mink, butterflies, rac-coons and foxes go about their normal daily activities. I added that sitting motionless in a thicket to learn about the behavior of wild animals and observe their natural spirits was quite exciting for a young boy who really wanted to be an Indian. My father listened to what I had to say and didn't see any harm being done so I continued to enjoy my river bottom expeditions.

The 1950's and early 1960's were wonderful times to raise children. Parents had few worries about kidnapping, child pornography and other things that commonly threaten kids today. I am lucky to have been a child when children were free to ride bicycles for miles, calmly sit alone on a bench at night outside a grocery store, play cowboys and Indians through the whole neighborhood while sporting Mohawk haircuts, camp alone in the river bottom to watch wildlife and dream of protecting citizens of Dodge City.

When I compare the play of children today with play 50 years ago, it is evident that Americans have lost a tremendous amount of freedom during the last five decades. Of course, important freedoms have been gained during the same time period but our our freedom also has suffered substantial losses. And to think that we let them go so easily.

CHAPTER 4

Our Mother

Every small child deserves a good mother. We Bresee children were extremely lucky because our mother was smart, witty, strong and independent-minded. She loved children and her clever and delightful view of the world turned most of their experiences into fun adventures.

Polly Prevented Parochial School

Our maternal grandmother was called "Nanny." Nanny cared for her two children and ran the family household in Houston, Texas. The family sat on their front porch after dinner on most evenings to chat with neighbors who strolled on the sidewalk. Before joining others on the porch, however, Nanny donned a fresh apron that was clean and starched.

Our maternal grandfather was called, "PaPa." He sailed from Germany for the United States as a boy. Shortly after boarding the boat, PaPa located a girl who spoke both German and English and learned basic English by the time the boat docked in Galveston Harbor, Texas. PaPa's oldest brother, Karl, lived in Houston and met PaPa at the harbor. Karl drove PaPa to Houston where he had secured an apartment for him, stocked the icebox and cupboards with plenty of food and paid the first two months rent. Then, Karl handed PaPa the key and immediately departed for Australia. Fourteen years passed before PaPa saw Karl again.

PaPa was an 18 year old boy who was in a new country for less than 24 hours when he found himself alone. He was asked many years later to explain how he dealt with that and he simply responded that he learned to speak English very quickly.

Not long after stepping onto American soil, PaPa toured a few cities and rated the beauty of each city's women using a scale of one-to-ten. Several years later, PaPa met a woman he wanted as a partner for the rest of his life. Even though they met relatively late in life, he and Nanny were married for more than sixty years. PaPa was a hard-working and reliable employee for Humble Oil Company and was lucky enough to keep his job through the Great Depression.

Unlike our grandmother, PaPa learned to relax and enjoy life. A source of pleasure for him was sharing a few bottles of cold beer with other men. One afternoon PaPa enjoyed several "cold ones" with sailors who recently entered the Port of Galveston. The men got to know each other as they exchanged stories for many hours.

The sailors had acquired a parrot in South America and feared trouble if they were caught transporting a wild animal from one country to another. They were anxious to find a home for the bird and eventually convinced PaPa to take the parrot off their hands. The sailors claimed the parrot could talk and PaPa reasoned that his young daughter and son would enjoy having friendly conversations with a talking bird.

The parrot quickly became a member of the family.

He often flew into the backyard to spend the day in plum and chinaberry trees before returning to his cage at nightfall. Several weeks had passed since he was brought home but the bird had not uttered a single word even though the whole family tried repeatedly to get him to talk. PaPa encouraged everyone to keep trying because he believed the sailors did not mislead him about the parrot's speaking ability. Family members continued to prompt the bird with every word they could imagine but the parrot didn't say one word in response.

My mother, a young girl at the time, finally said, "Polly." The bird immediately stood up straight with excitement in his eyes and loudly screeched, "You Son-Of-A-Bitch." All stood still while looking at each another in startled disbelief.

Her brother repeated the word "Polly" and the bird responded by harshly shrieking the phrase, "You Son-Of-A-Bitch" even more loudly than before. The word "Polly" was repeated several times and the bird screamed the same obscenity in response each time. As the weeks passed, family members searched for other words the parrot might recognize but it became evident that the sailors had taught him to speak only one phrase and he only spoke it when prompted by the word, "Polly."

My mother and her brother thought the bird's limited and obscene vocabulary was very funny. They told other kids in the neighborhood about the parrot and many children wanted to hear him screech his naughty phrase. My mother and her brother took advantage of their playmates' curiosity by charging them a nickel for the privilege of walking up to the parrot to say "Polly" and then hearing the bird shout, "You Son-Of-A-Bitch."

My mother, her brother and other children in the neighborhood attended public school close to home. Weekends frequently saw the children shucking their shoes to explore the mud and brackish water of numerous bayous within walking or bicycling distance of their home. Many happy hours were spent crabbing, shrimping and fishing. When the children returned from a bayou adventure, it was evident that they didn't look or smell like they had spent the day in church.

Nanny and PaPa's two kids were quite happy with their classmates and the public school but Nanny wanted her children to attend a parochial school. The two children thought the environment of the parochial school was rather humorless and believed they would not fit in. Nanny persisted, however, and eventually invited an official from the parochial school to their home to discuss admission. The two kids immediately began trying to think of ways to head-off their mother's plan.

When the admissions official arrived, the two children wiggled through dirt in the crawl space under their house to position themselves directly below the living room floor so they could hear the conversation between Nanny and the church official. When they heard specific plans being made to transfer the two kids to parochial school, the youngsters decided to take action.

Their house was small and the parrot was sitting in his cage on the back porch only a short distance from the living room. The kids remembered that the door between the porch and main part of the house was wide open so they wiggled through the crawl space to position themselves near the back porch. They prompted the parrot for the only phrase he knew by saying, "Polly." As expected, the parrot loudly screamed, "You Son-Of-A-Bitch!" The children quickly prompted the bird two more times and he loudly shrieked his phrase twice more. The kids quickly wiggled through the crawl space back to the living room floor to hear the adults.

They heard nothing but complete silence for a minute or two. It took Nanny that long to regain her composure enough to attempt to clarify the situation. She explained, "My husband drank a few cold ones with sailors who gave him an illegal parrot to talk with our two children." The church official listened in complete silence.

Nanny knew she had dug herself into a hole and continued grasping for an exit. She added, "The Parrot knows how to say 'You Son-Of-A-Bitch' really well so my children charge neighborhood kids money to hear him speak." The admissions official remained silent.

After another moment or two, a few brief words were exchanged and the official departed. As you might guess, my mother and her brother never received an invitation to attend the parochial school and they were quite pleased with the outcome. You have to agree that the two kids had learned at an early age to think on their feet or, more accurately, on their stomachs. My mother continues to exhibit that characteristic to this day.

Glamorous Girls In Hot Coats

Our mother has always been a smart, capable woman who can remain calm in the face of pressure. The following story will demonstrate those traits.

When she was eighteen years old in Houston, Texas, our mother worked as a secretary for a retail store and her friend, Cleo, worked as a dispatcher for the Police Department. World War II was underway and many consumer items were rationed. Most things were in short supply but a local department store still had a few fur coats. The two young women each wanted one.

Our mother earned $10.50 each week and Cleo's salary was similarly small so the price of a fur coat appeared to be out of reach. However, the store had "Will Call" so the young women purchased their coats by making a regular weekly remittance. It seemed to take forever to pay for the coats completely since only one or two dollars were remitted each week. However, the two women continued to make their small payments regularly and proudly owned the furs outright one June day.

A large event was scheduled for the very next Sunday afternoon at the Houston coliseum to raise money for the war effort. It was to be a formal affair that featured Hollywood stars so our mother and Cleo thought the event would be an excellent place to show their new coats. Of course, June in Houston, Texas, is very hot but the excitement of wearing their new furs was too much to resist. The girls worked for hours getting ready for the event. They tried to look as glamorous as possible and then rode the city bus downtown to a stop five blocks from the coliseum. They planned to look extremely swank as they strolled the last few blocks while wearing their new furs.

When the girls exited the bus, their excitement grew when they saw that the sidewalk was extremely crowded with people walking toward the coliseum. This was an appropriately large audience to appreciate their glamorous furs, they thought. They adjusted their clothing one more time to look slightly more elegant. The bottoms of their three-quarter length furs were aligned exactly with the hem of their dresses and fur-covered buttons were arranged perfectly. The two young women were ready to join the throng of people. They felt like a million dollars as they began to saunter slowly along the sidewalk.

However, they walked only one block when something unexpected occurred. Cleo's father worked for the Animal Control Department in Houston. He drove a rusty, beat-up, flatbed truck with wire cages piled high behind the cab. The cages were occupied with dogs and cats nearly to capacity when Cleo's father saw my mother and Cleo walking. He leaned out the truck window to shout and wave as he called them by name. Cleo immediately recognized her father's voice and turned toward my mother while sternly declaring, "Keep walking."

Cleo's dad began to honk the truck's horn in an attempt to get the girls attention. When he did that, the dogs and cats responded by emitting a cacophony of barks and a symphony of meows. His truck sounded like a ninety piece orchestra warming up before any of the instruments were tuned. Cleo turned toward my mother and hissed, "Whatever you do, don't turn around." Then she ordered, "Keep walking."

Cleo's father thought the girls couldn't hear him because of the huge crowd so he drove ahead to the next cross street and pulled over at the intersection. His truck partially blocked the crosswalk and people crowded around his vehicle while trying to cross the street. When my mother and Cleo approached the intersection, Cleo's dad made sure they heard him by honking the horn heavily and waving both hands as he shouted their names. This caused the dogs and cats to erupt into more barks and meows.

The crowd on the sidewalk recognized the man as an animal control officer and assumed that his unusual behavior was directed at animals on the sidewalk. Most of the people looked in the direction of his scrutiny but the only unusual thing they could see was two young women wearing fur coats in the June heat. Nearly everyone stopped and simply stared at the girls while waiting for their response. My mother and Cleo had no choice but to acknowledge the presence of Cleo's father.

As the crowd watched, the two young women reluctantly wiggled through the mass of onlookers to the truck. Most of the crowd remained stationary to learn what had attracted the attention of the animal control officer. They heard the man offer to give the girls a ride to the coliseum but Cleo crisply responded that they would rather walk and enjoy the fresh air. That response seemed to puzzle the crowd so they continued to watch.

Cleo's father noticed the people's perplexity so he remarked that the girls must be warm in their fur coats and insisted that they accept his offer of a ride. By that time, the bottleneck created by the truck obstructing the crosswalk caused the crowd to grow even larger and more attention was focused on the two girls wearing fur coats. Too embarrassed to remain on the sidewalk any longer, the two glamorous young women climbed into the cab of the beat-up old truck and it continued through the intersection at last.

As the coliseum came into sight, throngs of people in tuxedos and long dresses could be seen ascending the front steps of the building. The steps ended at a large area where more than a hundred people congregated to talk.

Embarrassed at the thought of people seeing them exit the beat-up flatbed truck, Cleo ordered, "Dad, pull to the back of the building so we can smoke before the show."

Cleo's father saw people smoking at the top of the stairs so he ignored her demand and stopped at the bottom of the steps in front of the building. Most people stopped talking and stared at the old truck carrying dozens of barking dogs and meowing cats along with two glamorous young women dressed in fur coats.

The two women were so embarrassed that they nearly stopped breathing. They slid off the truck seat as quickly as possible and immediately raced inside to distance themselves from the commotion. After hiding in a restroom for twenty minutes to regain their composure, the two young women joined the festivities and acted as cool as a couple of glamorous cucumbers. Their ability to regain their composure helped make the day a success in spite of an embarrassing situation.

Typing Tension

Another story illustrates how our mother has always been a smart and capable woman who can remain calm in the face of pressure.

When Pearl Harbor was bombed in 1941, U.S. factory production was redirected toward equipment and materials which supported the war effort. Warner and Swasey in Houston produced turret lathes and machine tool equipment so their business became very important when the war began. Our mother had recently landed what she viewed as her secretarial dream job at Warner and Swasey.

Hughes Tool Company in Houston wanted to purchase

turret lathes from Warner and Swasey to produce struts for U.S. war planes so a meeting was scheduled to prepare a prospectus for the U.S. government. The meeting was held in a large conference room at Hughes Tool Company and was attended by three principal groups of people. Howard Hughes flew to Houston for the meeting and was accompanied by Hughes Tool Company executives. The Warner and Swasey contingent included our mother, another secretary named Boots, several technical people and their boss. The third group consisted of several officials from Washington, D.C., who represented the U.S. government.

When the meeting began, the government officials stated that six copies of the prospectus must be typed without a single mistake and with no erasures. That was an enormous problem at that time because computers and self correcting typewriters did not exist so no mistakes could be tolerated. If a single typing mistake was made, all copies of the entire page were unusable and it needed to be typed again. Since the prospectus was composed of a large number of pages which contained technical jargon, typing was a daunting task.

Much tension was in the air and people grumbled about the strict typing demand. Howard Hughes angrily remarked that the meeting would have to continue for several days to satisfy the government's typing requirement. It was obvious that enormous pressure would fall on the typist and it was essential that she could remain cool under pressure.

That is why my mother was asked to attend the meeting. Her brand new electric typewriter was carried to the meeting and set up for her. Copy was written by hand and given to my mother for typing exactly as it was written.

When she finished typing a page and its copies, they were passed to Boots for examination and then handed to government officials who checked every word on all copies.

To everyone's amazement, my mother typed six copies of the entire prospectus without making a single mistake. The meeting ended much sooner than anyone had anticipated and everyone was happy to get back to other duties. When my mother arrived at work the next morning, two dozen roses decorated her desk along with a Thank You card from Howard Hughes. My mother's ability to remain cool under pressure certainly helped get a difficult war time job completed.

Calm During A Jailhouse Jam

This story illustrates how our mother can remain calm in the face of pressure. My mother learned the ways of children firsthand while growing up with her brother in Houston so it took an awful lot of child mischief to fluster her. Her calmness under pressure was evident one night when we watched a movie on television.

Our mother enjoyed good, hardy western movies. She had tried to watch a particular John Wayne television movie several times but was interrupted so often that she missed most of it and never got to see its ending. That particular movie was scheduled to be broadcast on television again and she was determined to watch it from beginning to end. She knew that I would enjoy the film and invited me to join her. We settled into the family room about fifteen minutes before the movie began to allow time to tune the television set for the best reception. We got a good signal and eagerly anticipated two hours of excellent entertainment.

Almost as soon as the movie started, the telephone rang and I ran into the hallway to answer it. The caller identified himself as a Vandalia Police Officer and stated that one of my younger brothers had been arrested for illegal possession of alcohol. He added that our mother needed to go to the jail and bail the boy out. I thanked the Officer and hung up the telephone.

I returned to the family room and my mother quickly summarized the part of the movie I missed while talking on the telephone. We continued watching the movie until the station paused for a commercial break and then my mother asked who had called. I informed her that it was the police, told her who was behind bars and added that he asked us to go to the jail and post bail. She calmly responded that she had waited a long time to see this particular John Wayne film and she was going to watch the whole thing. We continued to enjoy the movie for two more hours. When it ended, we had a lively discussion about our favorite parts and agreed that the movie had lived up to its good reputation.

We drove to the jailhouse and the policeman explained the situation to us. My brother and four other boys were arrested for illegal possession of beer and we needed to pay a small bail to release him from jail. He explained that the five boys had a six pack and each boy drank one can of beer. None of the boys wanted to drink the last beer and the remaining can led to their arrest for illegal possession of alcohol. Our mother and the policeman knew each other quite well and they chatted about many topics during the next half hour. She eventually posted bail and the officer lead us to the cell area.

The other four boys had departed several hours earlier because their parents rushed to the jail immediately upon learning of their arrest. When we entered the cell area, my brother sat alone in a cell looking forlorn and forgotten. He looked so pitiful that our mother did not make him endure a lecture when he was released.

Our mother had been to the jailhouse on other occasions to rescue her children and that was not such a big deal in those days. The Police Department focused on helping parents teach children good things rather than punishing kids. After seeing the kind of good men my brothers became, I think that the Police Department's strategy was effective and the policemen did their job well.

Mom's Cooking

Our mother worked hard every day to prepare nourishing meals for children in our family. Her dishes were nourishing but that doesn't mean they tasted delicious. Our mother always said that she hated to cook and did it only to provide her nine children with nourishment. In fact, she normally didn't eat her own cooking and that was easy to understand.

Her disinterest in cooking was reflected in her general approach to frying chicken. First, she filled three frying pans with cuts of chicken. Then, she set about working somewhere in the house until she smelled smoke. At that time, she returned to the kitchen and turned the chicken over. She immediately went back to work in the house until she smelled smoke again. Then, she returned to the kitchen once more and removed the chicken from the three frying pans before loading them with more chicken. This process continued for about two and a half hours.

As you might guess, we ate a lot of fried chicken that was totally black. We ate many dishes that were served black. Our mother's cooking was so bad that she could boil carrots and burn them because she lost track of time and the water boiled away. We were accustomed to eating burned food and more-or-less accepted that fried chicken, carrots, toast and many other things were supposed to be black. As we grew older and left home, we discovered that most of the dishes our mother had prepared were not supposed to be colored black.

Years later, several of my brothers decided to have some fun with our mother and her cooking. During a holiday visit home, the boys claimed that our mother's cooking caused a problem for them. One by one, every boy ejected gas from his lower torso when our mother was nearby. Each shot of gas was accompanied by an innocent-sounding apology and a claim that gas such as that was unusual.

Since all of the boys appeared to exhibit the same problem, our mother naturally tried to identify a common cause for it. Each boy claimed that he experienced this problem only when he visited home. Our mother quickly concluded that her cooking might be causing the difficulty. The boys replied that they didn't want to hurt her feelings but they believed that eating so much burned food indeed caused their gas problems.

Our mother believed the boys and felt badly. She had visions of her little children eating food that created intestinal problems and other ailments which would cause problems through their entire lives. The boys let her dangle in the breeze, so to speak, for another day or two before telling her that the whole gas episode was a prank.

Some people undoubtedly will feel sorry for our mother but you shouldn't do that because she pranked her own children pretty well. For example, I remember when she caused me to act foolishly on the telephone for nearly two years. She had just gotten "Caller Identification" for her telephone. "Caller ID" was quite new at that time and I had never heard of it.

When I called my mother one weekend, she picked-up the telephone after a few rings and said, "Hello, Randy." I replied, "How did you know it was me?" She said, "I can tell by the way the telephone rings." I asked, "The phone rings differently when I call than when others call?" She responded, "Yes" so I asked, "How is the ring different?" She said, "Oh, I can't describe it; it just is."

Well, we went through this same exchange each time I called for nearly two years. She had convinced me that her telephone somehow rang differently when I called her. Finally, a friend informed me about Caller ID and I realized that I had been pranked (again) by my own mother.

Expensive Binoculars

Parents sometimes go to extreme measures to help their children. When I was in the sixth grade I became interested in bird watching and my mother supported my interest by buying binoculars for my birthday. She paid twenty two dollars which was a lot of money in those days. A couple of years later, I needed some money and offered to sell her the binoculars. She remembered what she paid for them and gave me twenty two dollars.

Six months later, I needed binoculars for a Boy Scout project and my good mother gave me the binoculars as a Christmas gift. When I was a sophomore in high school about two years after that, I needed money for a big dance. Again, my mother repurchased the binoculars for twenty two dollars.

A few months later, she gave the binoculars to one of my brothers as a birthday present. Within a year, he needed money and sold them back to our mother. A couple of years later, I was planning a trip to the Rocky Mountains and asked her if she still had the binoculars. She gave them to me again as a gift. After being in college for several years, I needed to raise money to complete my degree and again my good mother purchased the binoculars for twenty two dollars.

Many years passed and I forgot all about them. When I was 52 years old, my mother surprised me with the same tired binoculars as a Christmas gift. She reminded me that she paid for them five times and added that she did not want to purchase them again. Of course, I wouldn't take ten thousand dollars for them now.

Volunteer Work

With nine children, our mother was actively involved in the local schools. While living in St. Louis, we attended a grade school which held a large event every year. One year, our mother was put in charge of fund raising during the event. Raising money was important for the school and she struggled to think of an effective way to achieve their fund raising goal. Even though she and others had brainstormed for a long time, they weren't satisfied with any of the ideas they had conceived.

The Saint Louis Cardinals baseball team has a long

and distinguished history in major league baseball and Saint Louis had become one of the most exciting baseball cities in the world. Newspapers frequently published stories about Cardinals players and their families and the Saint Louis Post-Dispatch had recently carried a story about Stan "The Man" Musial and his family. Our mother read the story and concluded that Stan's wife, Lillian, must be good at fund raising. In those days, nearly everyone was listed in the telephone book so our mother telephoned the Musial residence and asked Lillian for advice on raising money for the grade school.

Lillian offered several good ideas but one was especially intriguing. She noted that flowers from funeral homes sometimes were discarded or given to hospitals after a funeral service ended. Lillian indicated that our mother might be able to gather large bouquets of free flowers and break them into small bunches to sell at the school event.

Our mother and her friends thought that Lillian's idea sounded great. Several funeral homes agreed to donate flowers and people in the community were asked to clean food cans to use as "vases" for small bunches of flowers. On the day before the school event, men delivered huge quantities of flowers to our house and friends delivered boxes and boxes of cleaned food cans. Our mother and her friends divided the flowers into small bunches in our kitchen and placed them in the cans. On the day of the school event, my mother and other workers set up an outdoor table on the school grounds and sold flowers as fast as they could collect money. By the end of the event, all of the flowers were sold and they exceeded the fund raising goal.

Smart, strong women like Lillian Musial and our

mother contribute many ways to other people's lives. Society owes them a lot.

The Oyster Eating Contest

When I attended college, I lived cheaply out of necessity but still managed to enjoy a few of the finer things in life. An example of this occurred when my mother visited me while I was enrolled in Ph.D. school at Florida State University. She drove to Tallahassee with three young women named Cindy, Brenda and Gay who lived near my mother in Illinois. The five of us went to an oyster bar for drinks and conversation one evening and discovered that the bar offered large, beautiful Apalachicola oysters on the half shell for a good price. I knew that the brackish bay of the nearby Apalachicola River produced plump, sweet oysters that were some of the finest in the world. I always wanted to sample them and was delighted that we had an opportunity to taste the oysters which were originally used to make the famous dish, Oysters Rockefeller, at Antoine's Restaurant in New Orleans.

While growing up, I heard many stories about our mother's oyster-eating prowess. When we lived in Saint Louis, our parents often went out-on-the-town to socialize with other people. Evenings with others sometimes found my father proclaiming that his little wife could eat more raw oysters than anyone. Talk invariably led to more talk, money was waged and a contest began between our mother and some big, strong man.

Our mother told us that she never lost an oyster-eating contest and often made enough money from the wager to pay for our parent's entire evening. I never actually witnessed my mother consuming a large quantity of raw oysters but heard numerous stories about her feats through the years.

While the five of us sat in the oyster bar in Tallahassee, I discovered that one of the three young women, Cindy, was proud that she could consume a large quantity of tequila. I mulled over the situation for a few moments and then focused intently on Cindy's eyes while confidently stating that my mother could eat more plates of oysters than Cindy could drink shots of tequila. Cindy's eyes intensified as she boasted that I was incorrect. After a suitable amount of bravado was discharged by both of us, rules of the contest were defined and a wager was made. My mother would consume one dozen raw oysters for each double shot of tequila that Cindy consumed. The contest would continue until one of them quit and the quitter would pay for both the oysters and the tequila.

We ordered a double shot of tequila and a dozen oysters and the contest began. Another double shot and another dozen oysters were ordered. Then another. People in the bar began to show interest in the contest and I saw greenbacks piled on numerous tables nearby. It didn't take long and most people were betting on one contestant or the other. The drinking and eating continued.

My mother clearly slowed down while eating her fourth plate of oysters. I reminded myself that I never actually witnessed her eating a huge number of raw oysters and I began to wonder if her stories were really true. Half way through the plate, my mother paused and looked down as she placed both hands in her lap. I heard loud moans from patrons who had bet money on my mother. Cindy became more confident and I became more worried. None of us had a credit card and I wondered how my mother and I were going to pay for all those oysters and all that tequila.

After a brief rest my mother continued eating and finished the entire plate. Another dozen oysters and another double shot of tequila were ordered and Cindy began to look a little woozy. Another round was ordered and my mother made slurping sounds as she sucked each oyster off its shell. Cindy looked even woozier.

Another order came and my mother made little grunting sounds as she consumed the whole dozen in record time. Loud cheers filled the bar as people realized that her earlier slowdown had been a ruse. The cheers were accompanied by loud moans as people who bet on Cindy knew they were in trouble. There was more excitement in the bar than I've seen at a Super Bowl game. People gathered around our table and strained to watch each oyster slide down.

Another order came and my mother's eyes twinkled when she glanced at me while pulling the tray holding a dozen crustaceans closer to her. She confidently grabbed the first shell and tilted it up quickly while she slurped it down faster than ever. She slammed the shell down on the tray and reached for another. She let liquid drain from the corner of her mouth onto her chin while she grabbed one shell after another and slurped each faster than the previous one. I smiled confidently at that point and realized that my mother was indeed an artist.

Cindy simply stared at my mother in disbelief and stopped drinking. She sat motionless for several minutes while listening to the sound of oysters being inhaled. The young woman couldn't stand it any longer. She placed a hand over her mouth and ran to the restroom where she involuntarily forfeited the contest.

The oyster count was an unbelievable eight dozen (96) oysters. The bar erupted in a forte of boisterous cheers and the rowdy crowd jumped up and down while shaking each other's hands.

People covered their bets and many came to our table to shake my mother's hand. The bartender recorded the date, 6-13-78, and contest results on a bar napkin and patrons signed the napkin. My mother gave me the oyster bar napkin many years later and I framed it so it could be displayed on a wall with great pride. The napkin reminds me how impressed I have been with my mother on so many occasions. On this particular occasion, she was spectacular.

Watson And Watkins

Our mother learned how to have fun from her dad, PaPa. After her youngest child left home, our mother found many ways to enjoy life. She acquired a small dog which she named, "Watson," who provided her with much fun.

A friend from Kentucky named Watkins visited our mother with his wife when they passed through Illinois. The Watkins' stopped by one day with a large bottle of Rebel Yell Kentucky Bourbon to say hello and enjoy mint juleps. Shortly after they arrived, the three congregated at the kitchen table and began sipping the Southern elixir. Our mother was seated on one side of the table, the Watkins' were seated across from her and our mother's dog, Watson, found a comfortable spot underneath the table. It wasn't long before a substantial portion of Rebel Yell had been consumed.

Our mother noticed that Mr. Watkins was squirming in his chair so she tried to identify the source of his problem. Her dog, Watson, had the odd habit of crawling under the table, laying his head on a person's foot and then pressing down. She glanced under the table and saw that Mr. Watkins indeed appeared to be squirming because Watson pressed on the man's foot. Mr. Watkins kept moving his foot but Watson kept repositioning his head to reapply pressure.

My mother decided to intervene by calling Watson away from the man. However, the mint juleps were having an effect and she mixed up the names of Watson, her dog, and Watkins, the man. She ordered, "Watkins, get over here."

Mr. Watkins gazed across the table with a distressed but mostly blank stare as he attempted to figure out how to respond to her order.

Our mother hadn't realized her mistake but she could see that her guest was more distraught than before so she assumed that Watson was pressing the man's foot harder than ever. She sternly barked the order, "Watkins. I said to get over here." Mr. Watkins couldn't think of a response and he simply stared at our mother with a baffled expression on his face. She noticed that her guest was even more distressed now so she stood up and hit the table with her fist as she shouted, "Watkins. Get over here immediately."

At that point, everyone realized that she had confused Watkins with Watson. My mother fell back into her chair and everyone laughed so hard that tears rolled down their cheeks for twenty minutes. For many years after the incident, our mother and Mr. Watkins both laughed heartily when they remembered the incident that day.

CHAPTER 5

Our Father, Dick

Our family left Saint Louis in 1961 when I was a fifth grader and moved seventy miles across the Mississippi River to a small Illinois town named Vandalia. We left a big city and became part of a small Midwestern agricultural community. Our father always felt compelled to prove that he was right and the move to Illinois presented him with many opportunities to prove himself because his new playground included nearly two hundred acres of farm ground, livestock and heavy equipment. Few things in life provide as many opportunities to prove yourself as a farm with livestock and heavy equipment. That made life with our father interesting and the following stories illustrate that.

Daddy Lived Next Door

First, I need to explain why we called our father, "Dick." That practice began while we were little kids living in the city of Saint Louis. The Petersens lived next door and Mr. Petersen was called "Daddy" by Mrs. Petersen and their four children. We Bresee children believed that Mr. Petersen's name actually was Daddy so we also addressed him as Daddy.

On the other hand, our mother called our father

"Dick." When the oldest child, Farrar, was big enough to converse, she called our father "Dick." He thought about it for a moment and decided that he liked what he heard so he asked that all of the children call him by that. Consequently, all of the Bresee children called our mother "Mom," our father "Dick" and the man who lived next door, "Daddy." As you can imagine, this provided many good opportunities for humor.

Our father was a salesman for Phillips Petroleum Company in Saint Louis. Most sales in those days occurred in face-to-face meetings because email, cell phones, video conferencing, and many other technical gadgets did not exist. Face-to-face meetings occasionally took place at our house when a business client was invited for a home-cooked meal. It was amusing to observe the perplexed look on a client's face when he heard the Bresee children call the next door neighbor "Daddy" and the man living in our house "Dick." Most visitors cautiously probed the issue in an attempt to piece together enough information to interpret the references to Daddy and Dick. Most of them gently asked for information such as where each child was born. Only the bravest visitors eventually asked for a direct explanation.

Of course, our parents enjoyed watching their visitor's information gathering process and used it as an opportunity to learn about each visitor by how he approached the issue. On the rare occasions that a visitor was brave enough to request a direct explanation, our mother simply laughed and our father simply explained that his given name was Dick and it was reasonable for his children to use that name. However, most visitors remained puzzled and our parents enjoyed their confusion.

Wrestling The Big Ram

Shortly after moving to Vandalia, Dick purchased a 186 acre farm that was located seven miles east of town. We planted grain and kept about forty head of sheep. Our flock included a fine ram that was the largest one I had ever seen. The dude was something to be reckoned with. If you turned your back to him, he knocked you to the ground and you were likely to see stars. This happened to just about everyone who worked with the sheep. We all recognized that nature assigned the ram the responsibility to protect the ewes and we simply tried to avoid letting him get behind us. If we failed and the ram got the best of us, we blamed ourselves and simply tried harder to avoid him.

For Dick, the issue was personal. The ram's aggressiveness was a bone of contention with our father because he thought that the ewes belonged to him rather than the ram. Dick believed that the ram should defer to him.

One day, the sheep needed to be vaccinated and four of us herded the animals into a small corral. The sheep nervously huddled in a tight throng to learn what unknown fate awaited them. The big ram was especially uneasy and focused a lot of attention on us as we prepared to do our work. Our work began and we were careful not to turn our backs to the ram. Ewes were caught one-by-one and guided toward Dick who administered their vaccinations. After we worked about thirty five minutes, one worker was focused on catching a particular ewe that was especially adept at avoiding capture and the big ram stepped in. The man was nearly knocked silly. On that particular day the ram's aggressiveness seemed to irritate Dick more than usual.

Dick decided that he had enough and it was time to teach the ram a lesson. The rest of us didn't take Dick seriously at first but soon realized that he was determined to avenge the ram's aggressive charging. We tried to get Dick to understand that the ram was simply doing his job and following natural instincts. One worker argued that it was futile and foolish to attempt to teach the ram not to follow his natural instincts. That proved to be the wrong thing to say because it compelled our father to prove that he was right.

Dick defended his plan by turning to me and asking, "Have you ever heard of B. F. Skinner?" I responded that I thought Mr. Skinner was a scientist who made great strides in the field of psychology. Dick said that I was right and declared that he would employ Skinnerian psychology to teach the ram a lesson. We all stood in the corral while Dick lectured about the concept of stimulus-response training which was first described by the famous psychologist. He explained how Skinner repeatedly gave a dog delicious food immediately after speaking a single word in order to train the dog to salivate when the word was spoken. I was curious to see how Dick would use Skinner's stimulus-response method to teach the big ram to ignore nature's laws.

Dick instructed everyone to get out of his way so we walked to the edge of the corral and climbed onto the wooden fence where we could see the action. We knew we were in for some good entertainment. The ram attentively watched us and seemed to recognize that a challenge was imminent.

Our father sported a pretty large beer belly so the

big ram and Dick looked like two Sumo wrestlers as they squared off in the center of the corral. They stared at each other eye-to-eye as they circled one another. This continued for several minutes as Dick and the ram sized up their competition. Dick suddenly lunged forward but was met squarely by the ram and neither gained an advantage on the other. The ram lunged forward but was met squarely by Dick and, again, neither gained an advantage. Both combatants repeated the same move a few more times as each seemed to search for a weakness in his opponent's defense.

Without warning, Dick lunged forward and dove underneath the ram in an attempt to execute a takedown. Dick tried desperately to grab one of the big ram's legs to pull his opponent to the ground but the ram didn't allow that to happen. The ram shifted his considerable weight onto the leg Dick had grasped and the leg didn't move an inch. Dick held his grip and grunted as he pulled his opponent's leg harder but it didn't budge. The ram waited a few seconds and then kicked free.

The big ram looked strong, proud and determined. It appeared that the two gladiators were evenly matched. The three of us on the corral fence couldn't resist the temptation to have some fun at Dick's expense so we began to root for the big fellow as he stood his ground and stared at Dick. The blatant cheers and enthusiasm we showered on the ram infuriated our father and made him even more determined to teach the ram his lesson.

Dick attempted to execute his takedown move again but the ram was not fooled and kicked his leg free. Dick tried again and again but he couldn't budge the big boy.

I was so proud of the ram that I shouted encouragement to him as loudly as I could. The other two workers joined in and I'll bet you could hear our cheers a mile away. Of course, this incensed Dick and made him even more determined to win.

To properly appreciate the spectacle we were witnessing, you have to visualize the venue with more detail. Remember that forty sheep had been placed in the small corral for about an hour before the wrestling match began. The dirt had turned into mud as it became covered with sheep urine and manure. It was quite a sight to see Dick dive underneath the ram into mud, urine and manure as he tried to grab and hold onto the ram's slippery leg while the big boy struggled and kicked. The idea that Dick was attempting to teach the ram to ignore nature was convoluted enough but watching Dick slip and slide in the dirty corral made the scene too amusing for words.

Dick and the ram were just about equal in size and the battle continued for quite some time. Fatigue eventually set in and the movements of both combatants slowed with each passing minute. Dick finally managed to slide under his adversary and successfully pull a leg out from under the big fellow. The ram hit the dirt with a big thud and instantly knew he was in trouble.

Hoofs and hands flailed wildly as both contenders sprawled on the ground panting and struggling to gain an advantage over the other. Dick saw an opening and quickly wrapped his legs around his foe to restrain the big boy. While laying in the mud and manure they both paused for several minutes to gasp for breath. I have to give my father credit for sticking with his takedown strategy and eventually getting it to work successfully.

After Dick caught his breath, he wiggled into a better position to finish his task. While restraining his adversary with legs wrapped around the big boy, Dick placed one hand under the ram's jaw to hold his mouth closed and then placed his other hand over the ram's nose so he couldn't breathe.

Dick held his legs and hands in place for a few seconds and the ram panicked. Dick viewed the ram's panic as the negative response he desired so he let the ram go. According to Dick, he provided a negative response to the ram's aggressiveness and B. F. Skinner would acknowledge that the ram indeed had been taught his lesson.

Dick was exhausted so he declared victory and drove back to town. The rest of us remained to finish vaccinating the sheep. As you might guess, the ram's "lesson" was not a lasting one because he continued to protect his flock instinctively as he had done before.

It's Too Wet To Plow

While growing up in Vandalia, my brothers and I reported for work with our father's employees at 6:45 am on days we weren't in school. Some of his employees were farmers and others worked seasonal construction or operated big equipment. These were men you ought to listen to when they give advice about farming or using equipment.

We gathered early one morning to receive orders for the day and Dick said that we would plow the north field at the farm. The men immediately glanced at each another nervously and shuffled their feet tensely. Millard, my father's foreman, finally said, "Dick, we had two inches of rain day before yesterday. It's too wet. You can't plow today." Several of the men nodded in agreement.

When I saw hair bristle on the back of my father's neck I knew it would be a long day. Dick pondered Millard's comments for a moment and then ordered, "Burl, you and Randy drive the four-wheel drive pickup to the field. Take a long chain with you. Fred, load a tanker half full and take it to the field. Millard, take Roy and the tow truck to the field. Take plenty of chains. I'll meet all of you there shortly." Millard pleaded, "Dick. It's too wet. You can't plow today." Our father did not reply.

People scattered in various directions to do as they were told. It wasn't long before all workers waited at the north field near the big tractor, a Minneapolis Moline M5. As soon as Dick arrived he sent Roy to retrieve the UB tractor and me to retrieve the Case tractor in nearby fields. He instructed Burl to attach the two-bottom plow to the Minneapolis Moline M5. Everyone returned and Dick instructed Burl to drive into the field at the edge of the road and begin plowing. Burl stared at his feet with a blank look, rolled his shoulders and then silently climbed aboard the M5. He drove the tractor to the edge of the field and paused to lower the plow. Burl gave the tractor power but traveled only about fifty feet before becoming stuck in mud. Millard turned to Dick and insisted, "Dick. It's too wet. You can't plow."

Dick did not reply to Millard. Instead, he told Roy to get a chain and connect the UB tractor to the M5 tractor. Now we had the UB tractor chained to the M5 tractor which pulled a little two-bottom plow. Our father yelled to give the tractors power and they traveled only another twenty feet before both were stuck in mud.

Without hesitating, Dick told me to chain the Case tractor to the front of the UB tractor. Now we had the Case tractor chained to the UB tractor which was chained to the M5 tractor which pulled a little two-bottom plow. When Dick gave the order, we all applied power and pulled the plow about ten more feet.

We had no more tractors but we owned a powerful tow truck that got us out of tough jams on many occasions. Dick told Millard to pull the tow truck onto the slippery but firm soil of the dirt road next to the field and extend the winch cable to the Case tractor. Now we had the tow truck tied to the Case tractor which was chained to the UB tractor which was chained to the M5 tractor which pulled a little two-bottom plow. When Dick gave the signal, we all applied power. The tires of the winch truck had little grip on the muddy road and quickly slid toward the field. The plow didn't budge.

Without hesitating, Dick told Fred to park the heavy tanker truck in front of the winch truck and connect the two vehicles with a chain. The aim of this maneuver was to provide anchor weight to the tow truck to prevent it from sliding across the dirt road. Now, we had a tanker chained to the tow truck which was winched to the Case tractor which was chained to the UB tractor which was chained to the M5 tractor which was connected to a little two-bottom plow.

When everyone applied power this time, the plow began to move. We kept the equipment running hard for about one minute and pulled the plow about 50 feet until the end of the winch cable was reached. When no more winch cable was available, my father waved at us to stop. Then, Dick set his jaw and declared, "We plowed." I guess Dick won that battle.

For years, the north field contained a low spot where

big tractor wheels had burrowed through the soil that day. Water collected in the low spot and it remained wet for a long time each spring. For many years, we often found ourselves working around the wet spot as we tried to get the north field ready for spring planting.

He-he-he

Like nearly everyone, our father sometimes got things completely wrong and a humorous example of that involved one of my friends in Vandalia. While attending high school, I parked with my dates under a large oak tree on our farm. It was a safe place to spend private time with dates since the one-lane private road leading to the tree was the only way in or out of the farm. Some of my friends learned of the location and parked under the tree, too.

Dick left town most weekends so the coast usually was clear to spend time at the big oak tree. As one weekend approached, some of my friends asked if my father would be out-of-town during the weekend. I had learned to keep my eyes and ears open to learn about Dick's plans and reported to my friends that Dick was preparing to leave town as usual. Dick indeed departed as anticipated but it was a surprise when he returned unexpectedly late Saturday night and immediately drove to the farm. My fellow high school classmate, Ed Stringer, was parked with his date beneath the oak tree when he looked up and saw automobile lights coming toward them.

Most of my friends were apprehensive about interacting with my father and learned to identify his car. Ed immediately recognized that the car heading toward him was Dicks. Ed panicked . He told his date to lie on the floorboard of the car while he sat as low in the driver's seat as he could. Ed hoped that he wouldn't present enough of a view to Dick to be recognized but he would be positioned to drive away quickly if it was needed.

It took Dick a couple of minutes to drive to the oak tree. He saw the parked car and its steamy windows. Dick paused to record the car model and its license number before he continued driving toward the back of the farm. After my father drove well beyond Ed's parked car, Ed sped down the farm road, pulled onto the highway, hit the gas pedal and quickly disappeared. Ed told me about the incident later that evening.

Dick hadn't gotten a good look at anyone in the car since its windows were steamy so the only information he had was the car model and its license number. A few days later he knew that the registered owner of the car was Mary Stringer. Mary was Ed's mother but Dick didn't make the connection between them.

Dick knew Mary was a divorced woman who lived in town. He was convinced that he caught her necking beneath the old oak tree at his farm. Dick was thrilled. I heard him telling someone about the incident and he could hardly contain himself. I've never heard someone tell a story while uttering "he-he-he" so many times.

I watched Dick interact with Mary on a downtown sidewalk later that week. When Dick saw Mary he raced across the street and literally strutted over to face her. He grinned from ear-to-ear and almost danced in place. Dick was excited as he threw jab after jab at Mary in an effort to get a rise from her. I lost count of the number of "he-he-he's" that Dick wove between his comments as he cajoling her.

Mary Stringer simply stood in silence and stared at my father with bewilderment as she tried to comprehend his behavior. She never did understand what motivated Dick to act like he did.

I must have smiled for a week after witnessing the interaction between Dick and Mary. I never told my father that he completely misinterpreted the parking incident because it was much too entertaining to watch him strut with glee and repeat "he-he-he."

Which Way Is Up?

Just about everyone who interacted with Dick knew that there were four ways to do anything - the right way, the wrong way, the easy way and Dick's way. Dick went to great lengths to point out the fallacies of other people's actions and went to even greater lengths to demonstrate that his way was the correct way. Most people found those actions to be painfully exhausting.

A few brave souls thought Dick's excesses were entertaining and saw them as opportunities to have some fun. My brother-in-law, David, was one of those people. Dick had farm acreage which contained an old house that was occupied by my sister, Farrar, and David. David was a Southern California city man who had attitudes about things that were quite different from Nebraska-raised Dick. David enjoyed baiting Dick into lecturing him about how wrong David was about things because he was amused by Dick's diatribes about things that really didn't matter.

A barn was located near the house and David began building a corral off a side of the barn. Dick visited David and my sister on Wednesdays for lunch and one day Dick saw building materials piled next to the barn when he pulled off of the public road. It didn't take long before he asked David about the materials and David replied that he was constructing a corral so he could get a milk cow.

People who are familiar with milk cows know that they tie you to the farm every morning and every evening. With all of the things that life has to offer, few individuals are interested in such a big restriction to their life.

Of course, Dick assumed that the California man knew nothing about the demands of milk cows so Dick quickly launched into a sermon about the foolishness of owning one. David defended his decision and, as expected, that provoked Dick even more. Dick expanded his lecture to include the need for fencing, feeding, watering, veterinary care and numerous other things. Dick lectured and David listened.

David continued building his corral during the next few weeks and Dick continued his Wednesday lectures about the foolishness of owning a milk cow. Dick could not believe that David was going ahead with his plan in spite of Dick's informative lectures. No matter how ardently Dick argued against the project, David listened but continued to work on the corral.

David eventually began talking about the type of cow he was planning to acquire and Dick simply couldn't believe it. One Wednesday, David informed Dick that he had completed the corral and was planning to get his cow during the next few days. Dick departed after lunch shaking his head in disbelief.

As Dick pulled into the driveway the following Wednesday, he got a glimpse of a cow standing in David's new corral and couldn't believe what he saw. While eating lunch, David stated that he had gotten a cow and he wanted to show Dick his prize when their meal was concluded. Dick was silent.

After they finished lunch, David, Dick and my sister walked to the corral. When they got closer, Dick realized that the animal standing in the corral was merely a life-sized plastic replica of a cow. David reveled at his achievement. He had successfully baited Dick into lecturing extensively for weeks about the foolishness of getting a milk cow. David laughed heartily and Dick winced with anguish.

Most people standing in Dick's shoes would feel foolish. Dick simply started thinking about how to get even and he didn't need much time to come up with a plan. The following Wednesday, Dick pulled into the driveway at his normal time. Instead of parking beside the door of the house as usual, Dick backed his vehicle up to the corral. David and Farrar walked outside to see what Dick was up to but Dick said nothing as he unloaded a sledge hammer, several feet of heavy wire, two metal fence posts and a tall ladder.

Without uttering a word, Dick walked to the middle of the corral and pounded the two fence posts into the ground about two feet apart. While David and my sister watched, Dick secured the ladder to the fence posts with heavy wire. The ladder was planted in the middle of the corral and pointed straight up toward the empty sky. When Dick finished securing the ladder, he climbed over the corral fence, loaded the sledge hammer into his vehicle and walked toward the house. He still hadn't spoken a word.

David and my sister were baffled about Dick's ladder

since it reached upward toward nothing but the sky. They followed Dick into the house and sat down at the table to begin lunch. David finally asked Dick to explain his actions in the corral.

Dick replied that David's recent efforts to build a corral for a plastic cow made it apparent that David did not know which way was up. Dick said that he put the ladder in the corral to remind David that the way up was upward.

You've got to admit, that was a good one.

CHAPTER 6

Rural Kids Have the Best Playgrounds

Our family lived within the city limits of Vandalia and also owned a farm seven miles from town. We grew wheat, raised sheep and did many fun and foolish things at the farm. Some rural kids feel more deprived than city kids because of their physical isolation. However, rural kids have enormous playgrounds which provide opportunities for fun that city kids never dreamed about. I'll tell you a few stories to support this.

Fur Trapping

We built several small lakes on our farm and much play focused on them. In those days, trapping was a good way to earn extra money because animal fur was commonly used as clothing and fur prices were high. A large fur dealer located only sixteen miles from our home provided a convenient buyer of fur. Trappers didn't even have to skin their animals because the dealer employed professional skinners.

I trapped muskrats in the lakes on our farm as well as

the river and creeks near our home. Muskrats or "rats" as they were called are a serious pest for many landowners. They dig tunnels in dams and levees which create structural weakness so most landowners were happy when trappers reduced the muskrat population in their waterways.

I began trapping in Junior High School and continued through High School by rising very early in the morning to run my trap lines before school started. I enjoyed being out-of-doors during the quiet time of the day and looked forward to being in nature.

Since skinning muskrats was unnecessary I kept whole rats in our household freezer until it was filled and they were taken to the fur dealer. The dealer paid about $1.25 per rat and that was a lot of money in those days. Put in terms that were meaningful to me, one muskrat equaled one ticket to the movies.

While traveling to the fur dealer one Saturday morning I noticed a large furry animal lying on the highway pavement. Several vehicles had run over the animal and he was flat as a pancake. I noticed that the animal was a red fox and knew that fox fur brought high prices. Since I was on my way to sell fur, I retrieved the squashed animal to see if there was any value left in him.

I lingered as usual at the fur dealer since I nearly always saw and heard exciting things. I watched the animal skinners work and admired their skill as they removed fur from most animals in only one minute. I listened to the fur dealer take telephone calls from Canada, Alaska and Montana to buy the fur of animals that I had never seen. Seeing and hearing those things was very exciting for a boy who still dreamed of being an Indian.

I eventually made my way to the trading table and piled my treasures on it. The buyer quickly ran his hand over the muskrats and offered me the usual $1.25 for each one. I accepted the price and then he turned his attention to my squashed fox. I nearly fell over when he offered $34 for the fox. That was 27 movie tickets for an animal that had been flattened by numerous cars and trucks. I learned that picking up road kill is not such a bad thing after all.

My fur trapping efforts paid well during those years and provided most of my spending money.

I also hunted and trapped woodchucks or "groundhogs" as they were called to collect a bounty offered by the county. Groundhogs dig large burrows in fields and pastures which create dangerous obstacles. I've heard many stories of horses or cows damaging their legs after stepping into a groundhog hole. Groundhogs also consume a considerable amount of crops so our county offered a bounty to encourage people to reduce their population.

The bounty was collected by offering proof that a groundhog had been eliminated. Official proof was provided by presenting both ears to the county official. I must have carried 50 - 100 pair of ears downtown to earn additional spending money.

I rarely spoke about my trapping activities and always wondered if the girls I dated knew that our date was paid with money collected from "rats" and groundhog ears.

Goose Hunting

Our family farm supported much wildlife and provided opportunities for us to interact with the wildlife. An amusing example of that occurred one winter after our father purchased two Canadian geese as pets. The wing feathers of the geese were clipped to prevent them from flying away and Dick released them onto a lake on our farm. Unfortunately, Dick released the two geese on the lake the very day before duck and goose hunting season opened. And he didn't tell anyone what he did.

As it turned out, my little brother Nick decided to try his luck hunting for ducks and geese on the first day of the season. He fetched our father's own goose gun with a box of shells and arrived at the lake just before sunrise. When dawn began to break, little Nick was lying in the grass below the dam eagerly waiting to see if any waterfowl were present. When the light became bright enough to see, Nick slowly crawled up the face of the dam and peered through the tall grass. To his delight, he saw two Canadian honkers swimming on the lake.

Our father's gun was a long-barrel single-shot shotgun that could fire only one shot before reloading. Nick figured that the second goose would fly out of range before the gun could be reloaded for another shot. The geese didn't look anxious to fly away so Nick decided to lie in the grass and wait patiently for the two swimmers to become aligned in a way that provided a chance to get both with a single shot. Eventually, Nick got his chance and fired. His judgment was good and both geese were killed with one blast from Dick's old goose gun.

Nick was extremely excited about bagging not one, but two geese on his very first goose hunt. He recognized that killing both geese with a single shot provided a story to brag about. He retrieved the geese and hurried home. Little Nick ran into the house holding a dead goose by the neck in each hand. He bolted into the kitchen where our father and mother were sitting and beamed with pride as he held both of his prizes high in the air. Nick proudly boasted that he killed them with a single shot from Dick's goose gun.

To Nick's surprise, Dick did not look pleased. He stared at Nick's two birds and asked, "Where did you find the geese?" Nick replied, "On a lake at the farm." He added, "They were just swimming around and didn't seem anxious to fly away so I waited until I could get them both with one shot."

Dick couldn't really blame Nick for shooting his pet geese because Dick didn't inform anyone about his actions. Dick's plan to have pet geese on a lake at the farm didn't last 24 hours.

Heavy Equipment

Most farm kids learn to operate heavy farm equipment at a young age. Before I was old enough to drive legally on public roads, my father drove me to a work site early in the morning where he instructed me to plow, disk, move earth, build a dam or perform other tasks using big equipment. At the end of the day, he would pick me up and drive me back home. It is surprising that farm kids can learn so much about using heavy equipment at a young age.

However, the process of designing farm equipment can be underestimated. This was illustrated quite clearly one summer when our father wanted to purchase a land leveler to shave off high spots and fill low spots in some of our fields. He visited several farm equipment dealers and concluded that land levelers were overpriced.

Dick was not about to overpay for what appeared to

him to be a simple piece of equipment so he decided to fabricate his own leveler using mostly scrap steel and parts from abandoned equipment scattered about our farm. We gathered steel and equipment parts and delivered them to a welder in a nearby town.

Fabrication at the welding shop began and, when the leveler was completed, it was so large that we needed to transport it to the farm in several pieces and then reassemble it in the field. We began to have doubts that the behemoth would be usable. It simply looked too big and too heavy.

When it was time for the leveler's maiden voyage, our father recruited my younger brother Nick for the task. They coupled the leveler to our big tractor and Dick instructed Nick to "Put the tractor in Grandma and give her hell." That meant to shift the tractor's transmission into its lowest gear and open the engine's throttle to the maximum. Nick did what he was told to do and the weighty monstrosity slowly inched ahead. Dick shouted more orders and Nick did what he could. As the massive beast crawled forward, it began to sink into the soil under a pile of dirt accumulating at its front.

Dick shouted more orders and Nick did what he was told to do but it became obvious that the leveler would become buried if he continued. Nick stopped the tractor, climbed to the ground and shoveled about 1.5 cubic yards of dirt away from the front of the leveler. Nick climbed aboard the tractor and tried pulling the leveler another time but dirt quickly piled up again in front of the partially sunken equipment. Dick shouted orders again and Nick did what he could. Dick shouted more and Nick finally shouted back. Nick made a few comments about Dick's design that were obviously true but not helpful at the moment. They both said many more things in anger.

Nick continued pulling the leveler but it took only a few more minutes before the steel behemoth was buried under an enormous pile of dirt. Dick blamed Nick for not driving the tractor correctly. In return, Nick made more unflattering comments about Dick's equipment design. At any rate, the leveler's maiden voyage was terminated and the equipment was never used again.

After spending a lot of time and money trying to avoid purchasing an "overpriced" land leveler, we eventually bought one from a nearby farm equipment dealer. In a roundabout way I guess I'd have to agree that we did pay too much to get a leveler after all.

Farm equipment also can come in handy when trying to get out of a difficult situation. Vandalia had a small airport three miles from town which served as a flight center and an official weather data station. When I was 16 years old, I drove to the airport in my father's Pontiac to retrieve recent temperature data for our father's propane business.

That was a trip I had made many times in winter weather but the roads were particularly icy that day. I was traveling on a straight section of pavement that ran beside fields which were devoid of almost everything during the winter except wind, snow and mud. The only hint of people was the occasional house every mile or so along the road.

I decided to take advantage of the icy conditions to practice my steering and have some fun at the same time. I gunned the engine to put the car into a slide and then attempted to steer myself out of the situation. I succeeded at this maneuver several times and was proud of my driving skills. When I executed the next maneuver I didn't notice that the crown in the center of the road had become particularly high. All four wheels slid over the crown and I couldn't regain enough control to make the car climb back over it. The car slid toward the edge of the pavement and eventually glided into a ditch beside the road.

The ditch was three feet deep and filled with more than two feet of muddy water. The car came to an abrupt stop and water immediately seeped inside. The floorboard of Dick's Pontiac soon had six inches of muddy water on it. I climbed out of the car to survey the situation and knew it would be impossible to drive the car out of the ditch. I was worried that my father would never let me drive again and I felt sick to my stomach.

As I stood there contemplating my situation, I heard a door close at a house that was located about 500 feet away. The man standing on the front porch was staring at me so I walked toward him. As I approached his house, the man asked, "Are you one of Dick's boys?" I froze in my tracks and couldn't reply, knowing that I had been caught red handed. Just about everyone knows just about everyone else in a small rural town so kids can't get away with much. He again demanded, "Are you one of Dick's boys?"

I replied, "Yes" and then pleaded, "But please don't tell him what I did." The farmer told me that he had watched me drive down the road and slide deliberately on the ice. He said that anyone could see that I was likely to get into trouble. His voice trumpeted a considerable amount of disdain when he informed me that I shouldn't abuse someone else's equipment like I did. I agreed with him and told him so. Without saying another word, he turned away from me and walked toward his equipment shed. At that moment, I knew he would help me.

The man pulled the big door of his shed about twenty feet to the side and walked in. I watched as he started his big diesel tractor and gave it a few minutes to warm up while he wrapped a long chain around the tractor's draw bar. The man climbed aboard and drove toward the Pontiac while I ran as fast as I could behind the tractor in an effort to keep up. He backed his tractor near the rear of the Pontiac and instructed me to attach the chain to the car axle. I crawled through the water and mud to do as he instructed. In less than a minute, the car was pulled out of the ditch.

I thanked the farmer profusely and thanked his big tractor as well. He simply looked down briefly at me from his high seat and then drove back home without saying a word. The car started and I drove away, wondering what he would tell my father about the incident. I drove the muddy car to a friend's house where I did my best to clean and dry the exterior and the wet floorboard.

My father never noticed the damp floorboard and the farmer apparently didn't tell him about the incident. Luck was on my side that day and I became a lot more careful with other people's equipment after that.

While driving to the airport many times during the next 3-4 years I occasionally saw the farmer working in his fields. I waved hello as I passed and it felt good when he waved back. It sounds odd to say this but I enjoyed a strange kinship with him even though I never knew his name or spoke to him after the incident.

High School Dating

Dating in a rural community can be adventurous because interesting problems are sometimes encountered which require a little imagination to solve. Of course, problems also provide latitude for a little mischief.

As I mentioned previously, a one-lane gravel road wound through our 186 acre farm and passed by a large oak tree where I parked with high school dates. Several of my friends also parked under the tree with their dates. As more friends learned about the spot, it began to get congested and we devised a communication system to avoid one another and prevent our dates from detecting our efforts. Communication worked like this.

If one of us wished to park beneath the oak tree, the boy first took his date to the A&W Root Beer Drive-In. After ordering a large root beer in a plastic cup from the car hop, they drove to the farm. At the turn-in to the farm from the public highway, the boy quickly scanned the road surface for A&W cups. If none were seen, he threw his empty cup onto the gravel farm road and proceeded to the oak tree. If another boy drove to the farm in the mean time, he saw the previous boy's A&W cup at the farm entrance and knew that someone else was at the oak tree. Consequently, he drove away and returned later to check again.

As the first couple left the farm, the boy told his date that he shouldn't have thrown litter onto the road and he stopped to retrieve his A&W cup. This signaled that the tree was available to other boys who drove by later. We used this system countless times and I don't believe that many dates figured out our system. Our communication system worked great.

Farm kids sometimes drive vehicles that are a bit unusual. That certainly was the case for me. Our father had a large 1961 pickup truck which was used to carry heavy steel for his business. The one-ton chassis of the truck had heavy leaf springs that didn't engage unless the truck was carrying a heavy load. This created the bumpiest ride I have ever experienced in a vehicle unless it carried heavy cargo. The ride was so rough that nonstop bouncing was experienced while driving slowly on a smooth concrete roadway. I became accustomed to the truck's rough ride but girls I dated in high school sometimes experienced difficulty.

I washed the truck until it shined and filled it with gas before my first date with Ann. In those days, gasoline was inexpensive and high school kids commonly drove for hours up and down Main Street. After watching a movie, Ann and I drove through town like most kids but it wasn't long before she asked to be taken home. I asked her why she wanted to quit so early and she said she had bounced so much that she hurt.

This same scenario was repeated with the next girl I dated so I realized that I needed to do something about the rough ride or my dating career was going to be brief. I knew the truck would ride smoothly only when it carried heavy cargo so I searched for weighty items to put into the truck bed. I found a pile of large concrete blocks in a convenient location that would work just fine. My new procedure to prepare for a date involved cleaning the truck and then spending the better part of an hour loading about 100 large concrete blocks into the truck bed. The load effectively smoothed the ride and no other date asked to be taken home early.

Our town observed a twelve o'clock curfew for minors so I normally returned my date to her home a few minutes before midnight. Then, I drove back to the concrete block pile to unload the 100 blocks that I had loaded into the truck a few hours earlier. It took me nearly an hour to unload the blocks so I typically got home about 1:30 am. The 100 block loading and 100 block unloading procedure was repeated every time I went on a date since the truck had to be returned in its original condition in case it was needed for my father's business the next morning.

During the winter months, another task was added to my dating routine before I returned home. We raised sheep at our farm and sheep have a knack for selecting the worst location, worst time of the day, and worst weather to give birth to their lambs.

During the winter lambing season I typically took my date home at midnight, unloaded 100 concrete blocks from the truck and then drove to the farm to see if any ewes and newborn lambs needed help. This often involved walking to a windblown hilltop in the pasture to find a wet and cold newborn lamb and then carrying it to the barn where his shivering body was dried as much as possible. The lamb's mother followed and both were put in a pen inside the barn where they would be warm. I provided hay and fresh water to the pair.

On some occasions, I had to repeat this routine a second time if more than one ewe lambed that night. When this task was finished, I attempted to exit the farm to drive seven miles back home but terrible winter weather sometimes resulted in getting the truck stuck in mud. That required starting a tractor to pull the truck out of the mud and returning home quite late. If the tractor would not start, I walked seven miles back to town and arrived home in the wee hours of the morning. The local police never bothered me as I walked through town after curfew because they knew what I had been doing. Small towns are sensible like that.

Jug Fishing

In addition to fur trapping and hunting, our lakes provided our family with good fishing opportunities. My favorite angling technique has always been a method of nighttime fishing called jug fishing. This is a social event that is great fun if you do it with the right people. Here's how it works.

First, 50-100 gallon-sized milk jugs are collected and their caps are secured tightly on the jugs with duct tape. Then, a hook is attached to one end of a two-foot long leader and the other end is tied securely to the handle of the jug. When nighttime arrives, you get plenty of minnows and a strong flashlight and load everything into a boat. A minnow is put on each hook and the boat is paddled around the lake to distribute jugs in the water. Then, you sit quietly in the dark and wait for the action to begin.

There is one more important feature of jug fishing that some people will not understand. For the most part, humans are more intelligent than fish so it is only fair to give the fish a better chance by passing another type of jug among people in the boat. If enough liquid from that jug is consumed by the fishermen, the fish have a much better chance of avoiding capture. It's only fair.

The fishermen spend some time enjoying the nighttime as they reduce their intelligence to that of the fish. Then, the person sitting in the front of the boat shines the flashlight on each jug in the lake. When a fish becomes hooked, it pulls the jug through the water as it swims away. One person keeps the flashlight pointed at a moving jug while other people paddle as fast as they can to catch it as it races across the surface of the lake.

In principle, paddlers eventually position the boat beside the moving jug and one person reaches into the water to lift the jug and fish into the boat. If jug fishing is done properly, however, the intelligence of fishermen and fish are fairly evenly matched so fun often ensues. Laughter usually erupts when a surprise occurs such as when an eel, snapping turtle or alligator gar is pulled into the boat and lands between people's legs. Nights spent on the water jug fishing have been some of the most entertaining and enjoyable times I have experienced.

CHAPTER 7

Pranks

Our family has always derived great pleasure from playing a good prank. The pranks could be quite involved and sometimes could even be called works of art. Fortunately, we lived in a small town where public officials admired an especially good prank even if, strictly speaking, it broke a rule or minor law.

The Great Corn Harvest

A man and woman who lived next door to our house in Vandalia were practical people who owned a hardware store, drove a pickup truck and planted a large vegetable garden in the backyard every summer. Their garden contained only practical plants that were carefully arranged in long, straight, precisely-spaced rows. As part of their practical nature, they believed it was wasteful to apply water to a garden so their vegetable production decreased during dry summers. When a summer was extremely dry, their plants more-or-less completely stopped producing anything edible.

Our mother's gardening style was on the opposite end of the cultivation continuum. Her yard overflowed with beautiful flowers of all sizes, shapes and colors. There were no rows and her plants did not include a single vegetable. Oddly shaped flower beds were scattered quite randomly through the yard. Most of her flowers were annuals whose beauty was most abundant during mid-summer so she watered them generously, especially during dry spells. People from all over town drove past our yard to admire its beauty. Our mother's flowers looked truly spectacular.

Occasionally, the neighbor man politely scolded our mother for "wasting" so much water. To him, her use of water was especially difficult to comprehend since flowers couldn't be eaten. After telling her how unreasonable her gardening had become one summer, our mother replied that she had been thinking of adding some practical plants to her flower beds next year. He asked what she was planning to do and our mother replied that she would add one or two corn seeds to each flower bed in the backyard. She said that tall corn plants looked beautiful and would provide more variety to her flower arrangements. "Besides," she added, "I wouldn't mind eating fresh corn late in the summer."

The man launched into a lecture about the mechanics of plant pollination and emphasized that corn did not pollinate easily. He added that corn does not develop kernels on its ears unless many plants are grown close enough together to aid pollination. He asked her to look at the long, neat rows of crowded corn stalks in his vegetable garden as an example of how it should be done. He finished his lecture by pointedly informing our mother that she would not harvest a single edible ear of corn if only one or two stalks grew in each of her flower beds.

Now, our mother claims to be an original Texan and

she viewed his comments as a challenge. During the winter she studied corn growing and learned about hand-pollination. When the following spring arrived, the man next door planted his usual vegetables in his garden in the usual manner while our mother planted flowers in yet another set of random patterns. That year, she also planted one or two seeds of corn in each backyard flower bed as she told the neighbor she would do.

When her planting was completed, she walked to the fence and told her neighbor that she had planted everything as planned, including one or two corn seeds in each backyard flower bed. She added that her twelve corn plants would produce mighty tasty corn-on-the-cob later in the summer. The neighbor man remembered their previous conversation and laughed at her for stubbornly trying to do something that was certain to fail. Our mother simply said she would wait until later in the summer to see if her corn plants produced edible ears.

That summer was particularly dry. The neighbor's vegetables wilted and produced little edible food since they didn't water their plants. In particular, their corn plants were short and didn't look like they would produce a single small ear. On the other hand, our mother's plants loved the heat and sun and were especially appreciative of the water she provided. Her flowers looked spectacular, as usual. Her twelve corn plants soaked up the water she generously provided and grew to a height of nearly seven feet. Each corn stalk looked handsome and brandished the beginnings of several ears. The drought continued through the entire growing season and the neighbor's garden was a bust whereas our mother's beds were particularly gorgeous.

My mother has always been good at reading people's subtle body language and she felt that her next door neighbors especially condemned her watering activities that summer. They couldn't see our mother's corn plants since they were planted over the hill but they could see their tops and knew her corn was tall. The neighbor man commented that our mother's watering made her corn grow tall but he reminded her that corn can not produce kernels if it is not planted crowded rows that aid pollination. Unknown to the neighbors, our mother had repeatedly pollinated each corn plant by hand to assure that kernels were plentiful on the ears.

One evening, our mother saw her neighbors relaxing on their back porch after dinner and decided that the time was ripe to harvest her corn. She walked out of her back door with an empty bushel basket under an arm, passed close to the fence and remarked that it was time to pick her corn. The neighbor couple smiled politely without speaking but grinned and chatted as our mother descended over the hill into her backyard.

She picked every ear on her twelve corn stalks and filled her basket nearly three quarters full with large ears. After partly shucking a few ears on top to expose dense rows of meaty kernels, she carried the basket up the hill. She walked close to the fence so her neighbors could see that her basket contained fine ears with good-looking, fat kernels. They looked shocked at the quantity and quality of her harvest and didn't utter a single word. Our mother simply smiled and nodded as she carried the basket through the back door into her house.

Next, our devious mother quietly carried her basket

of corn out the front door and around the other side of the house where she dumped the ears on the ground near one of the corn plants. Then, she carried her empty bushel basket back inside the front door, confident that her neighbors didn't see a thing.

A few minutes later, she walked out her back door with the empty bushel basket. As she walked near the fence she told the neighbor couple that she wasn't able to carry all of her corn in one trip and she needed to pick more ears from her twelve plants.

The couple looked bewildered as our mother passed out of sight down the hill again. After a little time passed, she loaded her original ears of corn into the basket and walked up the hill. This time, the neighbors were anxiously watching for her to come into view. When they saw another basket of beautiful corn, they couldn't speak even though our mother politely remarked that her corn was looking real good and was plentiful.

She walked into her back door and then out the front door to deposit her ears in the backyard a second time. She smiled to herself as she stealthily reentered through the front door again. She waited a few minutes before walking out the back door with her empty bushel basket for the third time.

As she passed the fence she remarked, "Harvesting corn sure is an awful lot of work, even with only twelve plants." The neighbor's eyes were open really wide as our mother walked down the hill. She loaded her original ears into the basket a third time and headed back uphill. The neighbors were both leaning forward in their chairs anxiously watching for our mother as she trudged up the hill.

When they saw another bushel basket of corn, their eyes danced wildly but they still didn't utter a sound. My mother simply said hello.

She was having too much fun to resist another round trip so she emptied her basket in the backyard one more time and quietly reentered her house through the front door. A bit later, she walked out the back door with her empty bushel basket.

After stopping at the fence, our mother wiped the perspiration off her forehead and remarked, "I don't think I will grow corn next year because harvesting the ears is too much work." She added, "I'm sure glad that I didn't plant my corn close together as you advised because I don't know what I would do with all those ears if they had pollinated correctly."

She loaded up the same ears of corn for the last time and the neighbors looked shocked as our mother walked past them again. She told them that she was glad to finally finish harvesting and thought she would sit down to rest for an hour or so.

After she walked into the house for the last time, the man next door bolted to his pickup truck and, even though he lived next door and could easily have walked, he drove down the alley behind our mother's house to get a better look at her corn plants. His curiosity had gotten the best of him and that pleased my mother immensely. She would have paid a hundred dollars to hear what he told his wife after he counted only twelve corn plants scattered in the flower beds.

Ah, the corn harvest that year was beyond anyone's expectations.

Best School Prank Ever

Our mother prepared a hot meal for her family every evening and dining was a social occasion. Our father usually asked each child about school and most kids conversed happily about their activities. Our dinner table conversations taught us how to talk, debate, solve problems and become more informed about current affairs. It was difficult to get a word into the conversation at times. Eating dinner as a group was a great benefit to growing children.

Sometimes the whole family was involved in a clever caper. That was the case when I graduated from Vandalia Community High School in 1968. While eating dinner one evening a few weeks before graduation day, most family members were busy talking, as usual. I remarked that I was nearing the end of my stint as a Vandalia Vandal and I wanted to go out in a style that would make a true Vandal proud. I explained that I wanted to play a graduation prank on the high school but was having trouble thinking of a good caper which was not destructive. Almost immediately, ideas were thrown across the table like darts in a sports bar. Nearly everyone had an idea, including my youngest brothers and sisters who were barely in grade school.

It didn't take long before the idea was offered to raise a "Class of 1968" flag up the flag pole in front of the school. I replied that the school principal would never allow such a flag to remain atop the pole and it would be removed immediately. Our father raised an eyebrow and commented, "Why don't you put the flag up the pole so he can't remove it?" Given the principal's personality, the whole family, including the smallest children, began to get excited at that prospect.

I really liked the idea and said that it would be even

better if we could sign our names to the flag but do it in a way that provided deniability it things got out-of-hand in the aftermath. Everyone at the table tried to think of a way to accomplish that but no good ideas arose from the discussion. After a while, our mother suggested that we raise a Confederate Battle flag up the pole at the same time we raise the Class of 1968 flag.

Her idea was good because she had been intensely interested in Civil War history for most of her life and was an avid collector of Civil War artifacts. She visited local schools every year to show letters, cannon balls, uniforms, swords and other items while she lectured about the war. Consequently, everyone in the school system and most people in town connected our mother to the Civil War.

What made this idea particularly appealing was the stance that our mother adopted during her school lectures. The State of Illinois is known as the "Land of Lincoln" and was aligned with the North during the Civil War so our mother had a little fun by prominently voicing southern views during her lectures. She was known through the whole school system for telling numerous clever jokes at the North's expense during her lectures.

With our mother's reputation as a Civil War lecturer who poked fun at the North and me belonging to the graduating class of 1968, just about everyone in town would know exactly who was behind the prank. However, the flags still provided us with enough wiggle room to deny the prank, if necessary. As we pondered the caper at the dinner table, the entire family, including the smallest child, was really excited and we decided to make it happen.

Our mother immediately began sewing a huge Class of 1968 flag and an equally large Confederate Battle flag.

Our father and I immediately began to devise a way to raise the flags so they could not be removed easily. A quick trip to the school revealed that the only obstacle to our caper was a single pulley at the top of the flag pole. A plan was devised to cut the flag pole rope and then splice our flags to the rope with a hook and twine at one end of the cut rope. Then, we could use the existing rope to raise the flags to the top of the pole, pull the hook through the pulley and then break the twine so the rope fell to the ground but our flags remained hooked at the top of the pole. Within a few days, we had both flags and the means to raise them to the top of the flag pole and prevent them from being removed easily.

While developing the operational logistics for our project, we realized that a watchman was needed at a moderate distance from the flag pole to look for school or law enforcement officials. My entire family, including the smallest child, enthusiastically volunteered to stand watch. We also realized that two people were required at the base of the pole to rig the ropes and flags. I enlisted my best friend and fellow graduating senior, Dave Braun, to help at the flag pole base. Since our operation was planned for nighttime, we rehearsed our tasks at home blindfolded until Dave and I were confident that we could make the cuts, add the twine, tie proper knots and then leave our flags atop the pole. We were ready.

The night before the school graduation commencement ceremony, watches were synchronized and the whole family along with Dave squeezed into the family car to drive toward the high school about two miles away. When we were within a half mile of the school, Dave and I exited the car and made our way on foot to the school following the darkest route we could find. We laid flat on the ground at the base of the flag pole in front of the school and waited. Right on schedule, my father pulled onto the shoulder of the road at the north end of the schoolyard about an eighth of a mile from the flag pole.

At the appointed time, Dave and I began our work while the rest of the family sat in the car and scanned the area for anything that might jeopardize our operation. Not long after Dave and I began our work, we noticed that my father was flashing his parking lights. Flashing lights previously was established as a signal that a problem had arisen so Dave and I stopped our work and flattened ourselves against the ground in the darkness to wait and watch. A Vandalia police officer had been nearby and saw my father's car pull onto the shoulder of the road. He pulled his cruiser behind the family car, walked to the driver's window and asked, "Is there anything wrong, Dick?"

My father has the ability to think fast on his feet and he demonstrated it again when the police officer inquired about possible trouble. Dick muttered obscenities at the car while he pushed and pulled every knob on the dashboard (including the parking lights) as he pretended to be frustrated at the car. While moving his arms and hands from one knob to another, he bumped the automatic transmission lever with his forearm to nudge it into the "Drive" position so the starter would not engage. Dick continued to mutter obscenities while turning the key to start the car but it wouldn't start.

After operating the ploy for a minute or two, Dick looked directly at the officer and angrily complained that the car died and would not start. As the officer listened and watched, my crafty father gently bumped the transmission lever with his forearm to nudge it into the neutral position. When he turned the ignition key the next time, the engine started. Dick turned to the officer and said, "You'd better follow me home, Roy. I've got a bunch of kids in here and this piece of junk might die again."

At that point, Dave and I watched my father leading the only police car in town away from the scene and we knew we could complete our task without interruption. We continued our work, raised the two flags and pulled hard on the rope. As planned, the twine broke and the rope fell to the ground while our two flags remained atop the pole. We knew we succeeded and raced home to debrief the rest of the family. Everyone went to bed promptly so we could get an early start the next morning and see the fruit of our labor in the light of day.

The high school principal was a good man who tried hard to exercise full control of the school. Since our community was quite conservative, our two flags waving atop the flag pole suggested to townspeople that the principal was not in control of the school. The poor man felt tremendous pressure to remove the flags before they were seen by adults arriving for the graduation ceremony that evening.

Throughout the day, the principal tried desperately to remove the flags every way he could imagine. His frustration grew as the day wore on but successful removal eluded him. The end of the school day neared and only four hours remained before the graduation ceremony. The principal was desperate and called for a hook-and-ladder fire truck from a nearby community. The truck arrived only two hours before the graduation ceremony began and firemen removed our flags. However, the flags flew all day and many people in town saw them. The local newspaper published a photograph of the flags in its next issue a few days later.

By convention, graduating students reported to their home rooms to get organized for the commencement ceremony and I reported to Don Snyder's room. Don was the smartest and best teacher in the entire school and taught chemistry, physics and mathematics. Don had a sense of humor and a flexible mind so he naturally was curious about how the prank was accomplished. He readily recognized my mother's signature (the Confederate Battle flag).

Don instructed his students to sit at their desks and then asked if anyone in class knew how the flags were raised. He intently stared straight at me when he asked this question so I knew that he knew who pulled off the caper. I collected my thoughts and then replied that I didn't have any way of knowing for sure how the Vandals accomplished their deed because I hadn't seen it being done. That statement was technically correct since it was dark when we raised the flags.

Don's curiosity was about to get the best of him so I added, "I can think of one way that a person could have accomplished the deed, however." I walked to the blackboard and sketched the rigging while explaining how it "could have" been done. Don beamed with pride that one of his former physics students "could" have been involved in such a clever deed. I wish I had a photograph of the expression on his face.

Next, students formed a line in the hallway in alphabetical order about thirty minutes before the commencement ceremony formally began. That meant that my co-prankster, Braun, lined up immediately in front of me, Bresee. During the next twenty five minutes, the principal went through his traditional act of walking down the line and speaking kind words of encouragement to each student while shaking his hand.

Dave and I watched the principal approaching and we were concerned since he was extremely angry about the prank and had endured an extraordinarily frustrating day. We were confident that the principal recognized the Confederate Battle flag as my mother's signature but we did not know what he would do about it. We had visions of a variety of horrible punishments including not being able to graduate with the rest of our class. The principal continued to work his way along the line and then reached Dave. Surprisingly, he shook Dave's hand in a friendly manner and wished him well, apparently unaware that Dave had participated in the caper.

I nervously waited in line immediately behind Dave, wondering what would happen when the principal turned to me. At that instant, I felt an uncontrollable urge to have a bit more fun since these were my last few minutes as a Vandalia Vandal. When the principal turned away from Dave and toward me, I stared directly into his eyes and whistled "Dixie" with steady but barely audible tones.

Through the years, I have seen the principal angry on several occasions but I never witnessed anger like I did that evening. He stared silently at me with hatred in his eyes. I couldn't back down so I continued to whistle my melodic jab. The principal's face got red and steam seemed to shoot from every pore.

I expected the man to completely lose control. But he didn't. I probably was fortunate that we were in a hallway and our parents were seated only a short distance away.

Although the principal spoke kind words of encouragement to every other student, he just glared into my eyes with quiet, bitter anger. He shook every other student's hand but he did not extend his hand to me. He simply stood silently for a few moments before regaining his composure and turning away to extend a friendly greeting to the next student standing in line. I wish I had a photograph of the expression on the poor man's face.

We knew we had won big. We successfully executed the best prank our high school probably ever experienced. We feared legal repercussions and made a pact to not speak about the incident. I didn't speak of it again until I attended a class reunion 45 years later.

However, I celebrated our caper in a subtle way during our 5-year class reunion. The reunion was held at the local country club and I drove the same old beat-up heavy duty pickup truck that I drove in high school. To commemorate our flag-raising caper five years earlier, I attached small Class of 1968 and Confederate Battle flags to the radio antenna of the truck. I don't think anyone noticed the flags but I thought I had the best ride in the parking lot.

A Shinier Moon Never Shone

Many students in our high school class continued their education after high school graduation. A few months after beginning college, some of us were anxious to demonstrate our newly acquired worldliness to other members of the Vandalia class of 1968. Several of us returned to Vandalia for a weekend to boast about our newly acquired skills. A party was planned but, unfortunately, I was required to join my parents for dinner and did not arrive at the party until three hours after it began. That was enough time for eighteen year old kids to demonstrate that they learned to drink alcohol and they learned to get really drunk.

When I arrived at the party, everyone was hungry. In those days, there were no restaurants open late at night in Vandalia so we decided to drive eight miles to a neighboring town to eat at Mabel's Truck Stop. I volunteered to drive since no one else was in suitable condition. Eight people squeezed into my father's Pontiac and we worked our way to the edge of town where we hopped onto the highway. After crossing the river, the highway ran 1.5 miles through the river bottom along a stretch of road that was straight as an arrow and flat as a pancake. Immediately after entering this stretch, I pulled behind a pickup truck containing a high school girl and her parents.

We thought it would be hysterically funny to moon the girl so I pulled my father's Pontiac alongside the pickup and one of my passengers pulled down his pants to expose his bare bottom. The pickup truck slowed down and I slowed down. It sped up and I sped up. We remained directly beside the pickup and mooned for nearly all of the 1.5 mile stretch of road. I pulled ahead only when the highway climbed uphill out of the river bottom. We believed that we had just performed the best mooning event ever known to mankind.

Eighteen year old kids don't act very bright. While being overwhelmed with our clever deed, it never occurred to us that the occupants of the pickup truck recorded our license plate number and followed us to our destination. We arrived at Mabel's and ordered our usual "grease burgers" but never had a chance to eat them. A Highway Patrolman entered the restaurant and asked for the person driving the blue Pontiac to identify himself. I responded and he asked me to step outside.

The Patrolman told me that I was charged with indecent exposure, reckless driving, speeding, public endangerment and several other things. I replied that it was impossible for one person to do all of those things at the same time. The Patrolman pondered my comment for a moment and then responded that my argument was reasonable and he would throw the whole lot of us in jail. He told me to load my passengers into the car and follow him to the Vandalia jail. For the first time that evening, I was worried. It was past the midnight curfew and two minors were in our group. Fortunately, they escaped to the women's restroom when the Patrolman walked outside with me. The remainder of our group got into the car and we followed the Patrolman to the Vandalia jail.

My father believed that kids who got in trouble simply had too much spare time on their hands and he was known around town as someone who worked his teenagers long hours. He had recently attended a community meeting where he proposed that kids who get in trouble should be given a job working plenty of hours to fill their time. As I led our group through the Vandalia jailhouse door that night, I knew that I was the first kid in Vandalia to get in trouble after my father proposed his plan. Since the boys in our family worked longer hours than any teenagers I knew, the element of humor associated with the situation did not escape me.

We were placed in a cell while the Highway Patrolman briefed the Vandalia Policeman and they decided on a course of action. After about thirty five minutes, the Vandalia Policeman walked to our jail cell and informed us that there would be a line-up so the mother of the high school girl could identify the person who exposed himself to her daughter. The Policeman left to get the mother and arrange the line-up.

Nearly every situation has a bright side if you can recognize it and we found a way to add a humorous twist to our situation. When the Policeman departed, I gathered my co-conspirators and suggested that we should do the line-up properly. We agreed that our signal for action would be a count of three. The Policeman returned and asked us to form a straight line in the hallway outside the cells and we cooperated cheerfully. The mother was brought to the area to conduct her identification. As she studied our faces, I counted to three and we quickly turned and dropped our pants to provide a more appropriate view for her identification.

The result was hilarious. The mother shrieked, covered her mouth (but not her eyes) and seemed to shrivel to half her original size. The Policeman panicked and tried unsuccessfully to pull up the trousers of several of us boys. He kept pulling up boy's pants but they kept dropping them again. After a minute of mayhem, the Policeman turned his attention to the mother and quickly escorted her from the area. We boys pulled up our trousers and returned to our jail cell.

The Policeman informed us a short time later that the mother identified one young man as the person who had mooned her daughter. Don was charged with indecent exposure and the rest of us were allowed to go home. My heart sank because I knew Don had fairly strict parents who would be unable to appreciate the humor of the situation. I had a pretty good idea about what would happen next.

At daybreak the next morning, I looked out my bedroom window of my parent's house and, as expected, Don's father was waiting in his pickup truck in front of the house. I immediately got dressed and went outside. I said hello and Don's father responded only with, "What happened last night?"

I told him that Don did not moon anyone but he was identified incorrectly by the mother. He asked, "Who was the mooner?" I nervously mulled over the consequences of answering his question, knowing that another friend would be formally charged with a crime. However, I knew that Don did not do the deed and it was unfair for him to pay for another person's actions.

I gulped hard and revealed the true identity of the mooner. Don's father didn't utter a single word as he got into his pickup truck and drove away.

Roosters That Couldn't Crow

After graduating from college I moved onto rural property in Kansas where I raised many fabulous things including beautiful Rhode Island Red chickens. During a trip to Vandalia to visit my mother, I took two large roosters and four fine hens because my brother Frank was planning to visit Vandalia two weeks later to pick up the birds and take them to his home in Virginia. I left the chickens at my mother's house and returned home to Kansas.

An old ten foot by fourteen foot dog pen provided a

safe nighttime roosting place for the birds during their stay in Vandalia. Throughout the day, they foraged in our mother's yard and returned to their roost when darkness approached. As you might expect, the roosters celebrated the rising sun each morning. I think the sound of roosters singing is musical but their crowing really bothers some people.

A couple had lived next door to my mother for many years. The man had died and the woman lived alone in their house. Rather predictably, she complained about the noise made each morning by the crowing roosters. Our mother told her that the chickens were only temporary guests and all would be back to normal very soon. The neighbor woman didn't accept that and threatened to report our mother's fowl guests to the Police.

She never understood my mother's free spirit, sense of humor and lighthearted spunk. After her husband died, she became even more intolerant and my mother grew tired of the woman's attitude. It seemed like the time was ripe to have a little fun and even the score. The neighbor woman had aged and her vision was deteriorated. This, our mother concluded, was a weakness that could be exploited and a plan was quickly formulated.

My brother Frank arrived to pick up the six chickens on schedule. Meanwhile, our mother had gone to Wal-Mart to purchase six plastic chickens that were nearly the same size and color as her live guests. Immediately after Frank quietly loaded up the live chickens and departed for Virginia, our mother put the plastic chickens at various locations around her yard where her neighbor could see them. Our clever mother periodically moved the plastic birds during the day so it seemed as though they were foraging in her yard.

As predicted, it wasn't long before the neighbor came to the fence and complained about the birds. When she threatened to call the police, our mother told her to go ahead and call if she wished. About an hour later, the Police Chief knocked on our mother's door and informed her that there had been a complaint about chickens in her yard. He said the person specifically complained about loud crowing each morning.

My mother replied that it sounded like her next door neighbor might be the person who complained because the woman was getting pretty old and sometimes got awfully confused about things. She asked the Chief to follow her outside so she could show him what she was talking about.

As our mother and the Police Chief neared the plastic chickens, our mother pointed to them and shook her head as she said, "I bought these at Wal-Mart recently. They look pretty real and the poor woman next door thinks the rooster crows. Isn't that sad." The Chief shook his head, apologized for bothering my mother and immediately departed.

The Chief walked next door and had a discussion with the woman. He informed her that my mother did not have live chickens in her yard. The woman replied adamantly that she indeed saw live chickens and insisted that the roosters crowed at sunrise. The Chief responded that he personally saw the chickens and was confident that they were not real. He added that it was impossible for a plastic chicken to crow. The woman angrily replied that the chickens were real and the rooster did not crow when the Chief was there because it was mid-afternoon and roosters only crow at sunrise. When their conversation ended, the Police Chief departed and telephoned my mother to report his discussion with her neighbor. He added that he was worried about her and asked our mother to keep an eye on her neighbor. Our mother cheerfully agreed.

The next day, our mother moved her plastic chickens around her yard as she had done the previous day and the woman next door called the police again. A different Officer arrived and, as before, our mother showed him the plastic chickens and said that her neighbor seemed to be getting more confused each day. The Officer apologized and departed.

The neighbor woman came to the fence later that day and informed our mother that she didn't know how our mother managed to avoid the law but she vowed to keep calling the police until "those chickens are gone." Of course, our mother was delighted at the opportunity to prolong the torment of her neighbor.

Our mother continued to move the plastic chickens during the next few days and her neighbor continued to call the police every day. The Police stopped visiting my mother and began having long talks with the neighbor woman. Her grown sons soon began stopping by to visit their mother more regularly.

Revenge can be sweet. And fun, too.

Conclusion

This book illustrates that everyday experiences provide people with opportunities to inject a considerable amount of gusto into their lives. Stories teach us that we can approach daily living in ways that help us have bright, spirited and bold lives.

This is the first book in a series that recounts true stories of people who have approached life with unashamed zeal and the results are funny, educational and heart-warming. Please look for the release of other books in this series soon.

If you enjoyed this book, leave a review at your favorite book retailer and post a comment on your Facebook page or other social network.

Thank you for taking the time to read my book!

About The Author

A Midwesterner at heart, I was born in Oklahoma and raised in Missouri and Illinois. While a student in college, most of my classes were in chemistry, physics, mathematics and biology but I also made time for history, philosophy and art.

I worked for nearly thirty years as a university professor in the field of textile science at Kansas State University and the University of Tennessee. I also conducted forensic consulting for criminal cases that included the "Dingo Baby" murder case (Australia vs Chamberlain), the "Hillside Strangler" murder case (California vs Buono) and the "Atlanta Serial Child" murder case (Georgia vs Wayne Williams). In addition, I contributed insight to the question of image formation on the Shroud of Turin and conducted analysis of a historic fabric swatch believed to be from the coat Abraham Lincoln wore the night he was assassinated at Ford's Theater. Vacations from university work saw me using large-format black and white photography as a creative art medium.

I retired a few years ago and currently reside in Tennessee near the Great Smoky Mountains National Park where I write books, author a photography blog, photograph, enjoy fine wine and try to live life colorfully and boldly.

Connect With Randall R Bresee

Visit my Smashwords Author page to learn about future book releases: https://www.smashwords.com/profile/view/RandallRBresee

View my large-format black & white photographs: http://www.RandallRBreseePhoto.com

Read my blogs about making photographic art: http://Blog.RandallRBreseePhoto.com

25486398R00074

Made in the USA
Middletown, DE
01 November 2015